Machine and Deep Lear
for Content Extraction of Satellite Images

Manami Barthakur

Table of Contents

List of Abbreviations

- ANN : Artificial Neural Network

- ASDN : Adversarial Saliency Detection Network

- BP: Back Propagation

- BRBP: Bayesian Regulation Back-Propagation

- CAE: Contractive Autoencoder

- CGBP : Conjugate Gradient Back-Propagation with Polak-Ribiere updates

- CNN: Convolutional Neural Networks

- DL : Deep learning

- DNN : deep neural network

- E-SVM : Exemplar Support Vector Machine

- FCM: Fuzzy C-means

- FN: False Negative

- FP : False Positive

- GAN: Generative Adversarial Network

- GIS : Geographic Information Systems

- GMI: Geometric Moment Invariants

- IOU : Intersection Over Union

- KCM : K-Means Clustering

- KNN : K-Nearest Neighbour

- LMBP: Levenberg- Marquardt Back-Propagation

- MSRA : Microsoft Research Asia

- MLP: Multi Layer Perceptron

- MSE: Mean Square Error

- MSRS: Multi-Scale Relative Salience

- PCNN : Pulse Coupled Neural Network

- PCNN: Pulse Coupled Neural Network

- PLSOM: Parameterless Self Organizing MAP

- PolSAR : Polarimetric Synthetic Aperture Radar

- PNN : Probabilistic Neural Network

- RBF : Radial Basis Function

- RBP : Resilient back-propagation

- RoI: Region of Interests

- ReLU: Rectified Linear Unit

- SAE : Stacked Autoencoder

- SCG: Scaled conjugate Gradient

- SGD: Stochastic Gradient Decent

- SOFM : Modified Self Organizing Feature Map

- SOM : Soft Organizing Map

- SSI : Structural Similarity Index

- SVM : Support Vector Machines

- TN : True Negative

- TP : True Positive

- VHR : Very-High Resolution

- VSSOM : Variable Structure Self Organizing MAP

List of Tables

List of Figures

1

Introduction

1.1 Background

A versatile tool for exploring the Earth is remote sensing. Satellite images, also known as remotely sensed images, are the data recorded by sensors from a very small portion of the Earth's surface. In these images, to capture the spatial and spectral relations of objects and materials perceptible at a distance, different instruments or sensors are used. Satellite images are mainly used in Geographic Information Systems (GIS)[1]. The GIS systems which are used for classification are useful for cartography. The intensity of the pixels in satellite images with low resolution is enough to individually classify each of them. On the other hand, image classification for high-resolution images is more difficult, since the level of detail and the heterogeneity of the scenes are raised. The high-resolution images contain much information inside them. A lot of characteristics that are associated with nature may be there, in a satellite image such as color, shape, texture or structure, density [2] etc. The existing GIS extracts information from satellite images by adopting three basic processes. These are: i) identification of the region of interest (RoI), ii) object detection and iii) image segmentation [1]. The method of identifying RoI may be manual or automatic [3]. Similarly, classification systems use the basic recognition methods for low and high-resolution images. These systems give satisfactory results for low-resolution images, but with new high-resolution images, these same basic methods cannot provide satisfactory results. Now a days, to improve classification accuracy, scientists and researchers have made much effort towards the development of advanced classification approaches and techniques.

The process of partitioning an image into multiple segments is called image segmentation. The goal of image segmentation is to obtain a representation of an image with distinct partitions of common content with something meaningful. The representation should enable subsequent analysis. It is typically used to locate objects and boundaries in images. There are many approaches to segment an image such as intensity-based methods, discontinuity-based methods, similarity-based methods, clustering methods, graph-based methods, Pixon-based methods, hybrid methods [5] etc. Most of these methods rely upon the image characteristics these are measuring. Therefore, they work well in certain cases and not in others. For example, edge detection based image segmentation methods do not work well for images with ill-defined edges. Similarly, thresholding-based methods do not work well with images without any obvious peaks or with a broad layout and at valleys. Moreover, the images are usually corrupted by several artifacts, such as image noise, missing or occluded parts, image intensity inhomogeneity, or non-uniformity.

To classify different regions in satellite images, semantic segmentation is frequently used. Here, each pixel of an image is associated with a class of what the object is being represented [5]. It is essential for many image analysis tasks. The semantic segmentation differentiates between the objects of interest and their background or other objects. Semantic segmentation is also used in many applications such as autonomous driving, industrial inspection, medical imaging analysis, military reconnaissance, weather forecast, land use patterns, crop census, ocean resources and groundwater studies etc. [5].

An ideal algorithm of image segmentation is expected to segment objects which are unknown or new. Several approaches such as Semantic Texton Forest [6] and Random Forest-based classifiers [7] for semantic segmentation are reported in the literature. Many of these approaches depend on the characteristics of images that can be measured. For this reason, these methods work well in some of the cases and do not work well in others. Again, there are some unintentional alterations in the images due to noise, image intensity non-uniformity, missing or occluded portion in the image etc. Therefore, for segmentation in complex images, methods based on prior knowledge may be more suitable than other approaches. For these reasons, neuro-computing methods with learning algorithms have been applied a lot in the literature [8][9][10].

Presently, deep learning (DL) is becoming popular since it is very useful for real-world applications due to the efficiency and reliability it generates. Its work is based on in-depth learning of features and mapping these to probable output state. Most of the semantic segmentation problems are performed using deep networks, such as Convolutional Neural Networks (CNNs)[9][10][11]. In terms of efficiency and accuracy, these methods are surpassing other methods extensively.

Although, deep learning-based methods produce an efficient performance for semantic image segmentation, the models usually have a serious problem which is known as over-fitting [12]. Overfitting occurs when a deep learning-based model learns the details and the noise present in the training data to a limited degree may negatively impact the performance of the model when implemented on new data [13]. The reason behind the problem is that a huge amount of learnable parameters need to be trained by these methods and therefore, a large number of data for training is required. The problem of over-fitting will become severe if limited training data are used. For high-resolution satellite images, limited training data is a familiar problem as the collection of such images is either expensive or time demanding. Therefore, effective and new strategies for training deep learning-based models are required to overcome the problem of overfitting.

In this thesis, we explore a class of machine and deep learning approaches for content extraction from satellite images. First, we discuss the formulation of an Artificial Neural Network (ANN) based approach for satellite image segmentation in complex backgrounds. Next, we report a supervised approach for extraction of RoI as an aid to the learning aided segmentation methods. Subsequently, we experiment with a specific deep learning tool (popularly called SegNet) for image segmentation using the segmented image extracts obtained using a clustering approach. Then, after a detailed set of experiments performed using semi-supervised adversarial learning, we found that the combination of the segmentation network and discriminator networks as part of the Generative Adversarial Network (GAN) is most effective in extracting content from satellite images. Finally, experiments were also performed for better accuracy of extraction of satellite images by removing the noise present inherently in the images with deep learning-based networks.

1.2   Literature Review

Several methods have been reported in the literature for machine and deep learning-based image segmentation. Some of the previously done work is discussed in the following sub-sections.

1.2.1 Review on the methods of image segmentation based on machine learning

In this section, a detailed study of the literature related to machine learning-based image segmentation is presented.

1. An ANN architecture has been developed for RoI segmentation of fingerprint images in [14] where the authors trained ANNs with 10000 samples extracted from 20 fingerprint images.

2. S. Arumugadevi et.al. in [15] have proposed a method in which supervised feed-forward ANN has been trained where the labels obtained from the clustering method Fuzzy C-means (FCM) are used as a target.

3. In [16], Backpropagation ANN has been reported to get iterative calculations of image pixel for image segmentation.

4. An unsupervised, non-parametric method using Variable Structure Self Organizing MAP (VSSOM) and Parameterless Self Organizing MAP (PLSOM) is reported in [17].

5. P. Upadhyay et. al. [18] have proposed a method using Modified Self Organizing Feature Map (SOFM) ANN. The modified SOFM ANN has an extra layer of neurons for the specific application.

6. C. Wang et.al. [19] develop a method an image segmentation method based on Pulse Coupled Neural Network (PCNN) and Independent Component Analysis (ICA).

7. The authors in [20] have reported the development of a method for segmentation using PCNN where a combination of 1-dimensional Maximal Correlative Criterion with 2-dimensional Maximal Correlative Criterion to estimate neuron parameters forms the core of the work.

8. In [21], ANN-based segmentation method for a lesion in brain MRI where training has been done using gray levels and extracted statistical features from the training data with the labeled ground truth.

9. M. J. Moghaddam et.al. [22] has reported a method of segmentation where deep brain structures have been segmented using Geometric Moment Invariants (GMIs) and MLP ANNs.

10. In [23], a method for leukocyte image segmentation has been developed where feed-forward ANN with random weights is employed to classify all the pixels in a leukocyte image. Then, according to the classification results, the regions of the nucleus and cytoplasm are extracted, respectively, to achieve the segmentation.

11. In [4], automatic segmentation of the cell nuclei on cytology pleural effusion images have been presented. At first, contrast-limited adaptive histogram equalization (CLAHE) is used to enhance the quality of the image. Then ANN is used for pixel classification. Morphological operations are used then to refine the boundaries of the extracted cell nuclei regions. Finally, using the marker-controlled watershed method the overlapped or touched nuclei are identified.

12. In[24], a method to derive the colors, shapes, textures, or any other information from a satellite image using texture filters and ANNs has been presented. Depending on the number of textures detected in the image, textures are then placed into a number of sets,

13. In [25], the authors have developed different advanced image segmentation methods such as Cloud Basis Functions (CBFs) Neural Networks, ANN and Support Vector Machines (SVM) for remotely sensed image segmentation to get better accuracy.

14. In [26], multiobjective fuzzy clustering scheme has been combined with ANN-based probabilistic classifier to yield better performance. The multiobjective method is first used for a set of non-dominated solutions. A part of these solutions having a high confidence level is then used to train the ANN classifier.

15. The authors in [27] compare the methods based on SOM, SOM combined with GA, and some of the variants of SOM like the Variable Structure SOM (VSSOM), Parameterless SOM (PLSOM). Then an unsupervised and nonparametric method was developed by combining the advantages of VSSOM and PLSOM.

16. In [28], the authors have proposed a kind of supervised classification - SVM to segment magnetic resonance image (MRI). As a classifier, SVM can employ the structural risk minimization principle and perform better in segmentation tasks.

17. The authors in [29] have developed a method of image segmentation based on SVM. At first, frame difference combined with the morphology of mathematics is applied to extract the object roughly. Then, the gray value of image pixels and DCT parameters are computed as the characters of the image for training SVM. Finally, a hierarchical decomposed SVM binary decision tree is used for classification. Experimental results show that the algorithm is effective and robust.

18. In [30], a SVM-based method to automatically segment brain MRI images has been developed. The images are taken under two categories, either normal or abnormal brain which refers to a brain tumor.

19. In [31], the authors have developed a method of relevance feedback based on SVM. An SVM classifier can be trained with training data of relevant images and irrelevance images marked by users.

20. The authors in [32] have presented two methods for the evaluation of the segmentation algorithm which are Local Consistency Error (LCE) and boundary matching. These methods are used to evaluate segmentation algorithms based on SVM.

21. In [33], the authors have presented a method to improve the accuracy of clothing segmentation based on Histogram of Oriented Gradients (HOG) features and Exemplar Support Vector Machine (E-SVM) classifier.

22. In [34], a method to separate and segment objects of rice samples based on color and texture features and ML techniques is presented. Local Binary Pattern (LBP) texture feature and color features extracted from segmented images. These features are used to predict the rice sample objects using Linear Kernel-based Support Vector Machine (SVM).

23. In [35], a method for a fingerprint image segmentation algorithm based on SVM has been reported. At first, the image is partitioned into 12 times 12 blocks and the low gray variance background blocks are segmented by the contrast. The blocks that can not be decided by the first segmentation are segmented by an SVM classifier.

24. The authors in [36] report a method for the segmentation of synthetic aperture radar (SAR) images. The method integrates the use of multi-scale technology, mixed-model information, and SVM.

25. The authors in [37] have discussed a method for adaptive segmentation of aerial images. The adaptive segmentation is based on image segmentation through Radial Basis Function (RBF) neural network classifier.

26. In [38], the authors have outlined the development of an image segmentation scheme using higher-order image statistics and RBF neural networks. Then a classifier based on RBF neural networks is used to segment the fake and real images.

27. In [39], a method for segmentation of medical images of the brain by using a self-adaptive RBF-NN is developed. It imposes a confidence measure to select a subset of the RBFs in the hidden layer for producing outputs at the output layer, thereby making the network self-adaptive.

28. The authors in [40] developed a SOM ANN and RBF network-based work. A modular RBF (MRBF) neural network is proposed to improve the classification rate and speed up the training time.

29. In [41], the authors have developed a novel method for CT head image automatic segmentation. The images are obtained from patients having a spontaneous intra-cerebral brain hemorrhage (ICH).

30. In[42], an RBF neural network with fuzzy initialization and graph-based discrete approach has been proposed, for microscopic image segmenting and classification.

A detailed study for image segmentation based on machine learning methods is presented above. The methods use various ML classifiers such as ANN, SVM, SOM, RBF, etc. These methods use prior knowledge-based methods and therefore give better results than the traditional segmentation techniques.

1.2.2 Review of the methods of image segmentation based on deep learning

In the following section, a detailed study of the literature related to DL-based image segmentation methods is presented.

1. A. S. Parihar et. al. [43] report an approach for segmentation of satellite images. The proposed algorithm performs efficient segmentation by considering various aspects of satellite images like the Hughes phenomenon, the high correlation between spectral

bands, etc. The proposed approach adopts a clustering-based segmentation method that partitions image into different regions which represent a land cover map. It uses type 2 fuzzy systems and differential evolution for producing accurate and precise segments. The proposed approach algorithm requires the number of clusters to be specified beforehand. The proposed algorithm was validated by comparing the value of cluster validity indexes, silhouette index with well-known algorithms.

2. S. Ghassemi et.al. [44] address the problem of training a Convolutional Neural Network (CNN) for satellite image segmentation in emergency situations where response time constraints prevent training the network from scratch. Such a case is particularly challenging due to the large intra-class statistics variations between training images and images to be segmented captured at different locations by different sensors. The work proposed a convolutional encoder-decoder network architecture where the encoder builds upon a residual architecture. The work had shown that the proposed architecture enables learning features suitable to generalize the learning process across images with different statistics. Their architecture can accurately segment images that have no reference in the training set, whereas a minimal refinement of the trained network significantly boosts the segmentation accuracy.

3. J. Long et.al. [45] reports the development of a "fully convolutional" network which with efficient inference and learning can produce correspondingly-sized output by taking input of arbitrary size. It has been applied to spatially dense prediction tasks, deep classification networks (GoogLeNet [46], VGG net [114], and AlexNet [10]) and converted them into fully CNN. Using fine-tuning [47] they transferred learned representations to the segmentation task.

4. V. Badrinarayanan et.al. [8] presents a deep fully CNN. The network developed for semantic pixel-wise segmentation has been termed SegNet. It has an encoder network

and a corresponding decoder network. The encoder and decoder is followed by a pixel-wise classification layer.

5. O. Ronneberger et.al. [48] developed a method based on deep learning for biomedical image segmentation which has been termed as U-Net. It has been modified and extended to the fully CNN [45] architecture such that the network works with a very less number of training images to give more precise segmentation.

6. A. Yoshihara et. al. [49] report a semantic segmentation method for satellite images using the fully convolutional network. The architecture of the network comprises an encoder network followed by a corresponding decoder network like [48],[50]. The input size to the network has been changed from the employed value in [50] to 256×256. The encoder network architecture was the same as a convolutional network.

7. J. Patravali et. al. in [51] report a 2D and 3D segmentation method for fully automated segmentation of cardiac MR image. The method is based on CNN. It includes a 2D segmentation model architecture as in [48].

8. M. Langkvist et.al. [52] introduce a CNN-based approach for per-pixel classification of satellite images.

9. S. Jegou et. al. in [50] extend the DenseNet architecture [53] for semantic segmentation. The extended network into fully convolutional networks (FC-DenseNets), while reducing the feature map explosion.

10. A. Chaurasia et. al [54] has proposed a DNN (LinkNet) which allows it to learn without any significant increase in the number of parameters. The proposed DNN architecture attempted to efficiently share the information learned by the encoder with the decoder after each downsampling block.

11. In [55], K. He et. al. report the Mask R-CNN architecture which has been an extension of popular Faster R-CNN architecture. The developed architecture is formulated by changing required parameters to perform semantic segmentation.

12. H. Zhao et. al. [56] exploited the capability of global context information by different-region-based context aggregation through their pyramid pooling module together with the proposed pyramid scene parsing network (PSPNet). Their global prior representation has been effective to produce proper quality results on the scene parsing task, while PSPNet provides a superior framework for pixel-level prediction. The proposed approach achieves state-of-the-art performance on various datasets. It came first in ImageNet scene parsing challenge 2016, PASCAL VOC 2012 benchmark, and Cityscapes benchmark. A single PSPNet yielded mIoU accuracy 85.4% on PASCAL VOC 2012 and accuracy 80.2% on Cityscapes.

13. In [57], the authors report an automatic semantic segmentation method in satellite images without losing the significant data using SOMs and deep residual network. They have also developed an algorithm to find cluster boundaries using the particle swarm optimization technique (PSO).

14. The authors in [58] report cloud segmentation method using an encoder-decoder CNN. The method reduces the resource consumption by CNN while preserving its classification accuracy.

15. In [59], the authors have reported a method of super pixel-level classification and semantic segmentation for clouds in satellite images. The method classifies four regions such as thick cloud, cirrus cloud, building, and other cultures using CNN and deep forest.

16. In [60], a method to transfer learning capabilities of FCNs to slum mapping in various satellite images has been reported. The model trained on very high-resolution optical satellite imagery from QuickBird is transferred to Sentinel-2 and TerraSAR-X data.

17. In [61], the authors report segmentation method for a CloudPeru2 dataset using a CNN based on the Deeplab v3+ architecture.

18. The authors in [62] report an approach for road segmentation using fully convolutional neural networks (FCNNs) in SAR images.

19. In [63], presented a convolutional encoder-decoder network-based method in a wider range of satellite images to learn visual representations.

20. In [64], a deep learning technique for automatic extraction of valuable information from large-sized satellite image data is presented. The method is based on two architectures of convolutional neural networks called SegNet and U-Net.

21. In [65], a dilation-LinkNet (AD-LinkNet)neural network that adopts encoder-decoder structure, serial-parallel combination dilated convolution, channel-wise attention mechanism, and pre-trained encoder for semantic segmentation is presented.

22. In [66], a pre-trained AlexNet based semantic segmentation method is discussed. The network has been used to generate deep features and then the Conditional random field (CRF) has been used to achieve image semantic segmentation.

23. The authors [67] report an image segmentation method where they had shown that in their method features extracted from generic CNN architectures are used in an image labeling algorithm that does not require training.

24. The authors [68] report a DL-based interactive segmentation framework by using CNNs into a bounding box and scribble-based segmentation pipeline. The method

has used image-specific fine-tuning to make a CNN model adaptive to a specific test image, which can be either unsupervised or supervised.

25. In [69], a method for dual image segmentation (DIS) has been introduced in which label maps and tags from images are generated, and using these predicted maps images are reconstructed.

26. In [70], image segmentation method based on deep learning features and community detection have been reported. the method has used a pre-trained CNN to extract the deep learning features of the image.

27. The authors in [71] report a preprocessing method such as wavelet denoising to extract the accurate contours of different tissues such as a skull, cerebrospinal fluid (CSF), grey matter (GM), and white matter (WM) on 5 MRI head image datasets. Then automatic image segmentation with deep learning by using a convolutional neural network has been performed.

28. In [72], a deep convolutional neural network for semantic image segmentation has been reported. The approach separates an input image into multiple regions corresponding to predefined object classes. The authors have used an encoder-decoder structure to improve the convergence speed and segmentation accuracy.

29. In [73], the authors report an image segmentation system based on deep convolutional neural networks to contour the lesions of soft tissue sarcomas using multimodal images, including magnetic resonance imaging, computed tomography, and positron emission tomography.

30. The authors in [74], have reported deep-learning techniques for medical image segmentation. In their method, they have used fully convolutional neural networks (FCNNs) for image segmentation.

31. In [75] a multiscale convolutional neural network (CNN) model for SAR image semantic segmentation has been reported. The multi-scale CNN model includes noise removal stage, convolutional stage, feature concatenation stage, and classification stage.

A detailed study for DL-based image segmentation is reported above. The methods use various DL classifiers such as CNN, SegNet, AlexNet, Deeplab etc. These methods also use prior knowledge based methods and reliable in terms of accuracy.

1.2.3   Review of methods of image segmentation based on adversarial learning

In the following section, a detailed study of the literature related to adversarial learning-based image segmentation is presented.

1. B. Benjdira et. Al in [117] develop a method where the authors address the issue of domain adaption in semantic segmentation of aerial images and reduce the domain shift impact using GANs.

2. P. Luc et. Al. [118] propose an adversarial training approach to detect and correct higher-order inconsistencies between ground truth segmentation maps and the ones produced by the segmentation net.

3. In [119], N. Souly et.al. propose a semi-supervised method for semantic segmentation using GAN to address this lack of annotations.

4. W.C. Hung et.al. in [120] proposed an adversarial learning method for semi-supervised semantic segmentation. They design a discriminator in a fully convolutional form. It differentiates the predicted probability maps from the ground truth segmentation distribution with the consideration of the spatial resolution.

5. In [76], a GAN-based method where two networks competing with each other to generate the best image segmentation is reported. In order to perform a fair comparison with baselines and quantitative and objective evaluations of the proposed approaches, suitable two databases are used for the purpose.

6. In [77], the author describes a semantic segmentation framework MS-GAN to localize MS lesions in multimodal brain magnetic resonance imaging (MRI), which consists of one multimodal encoder-decoder generator G and multiple discriminators D corresponding to the multiple input modalities.

7. The authors in [78] have described a novel transfer-learning framework using generative adversarial networks (cC-GAN) for robust segmentation of different HEp-2 datasets. The proposed cC-GAN tries to solve the overfitting problem of most deep learning networks and improves their transfer-capacity.

8. In [79], the authors reported a semi-supervised approach to deal with the problem of image segmentation. The method uses the discriminator (D) of a Generative Adversarial Network (GAN) as the final classifier, and D is trained using both labeled and unlabeled data.

9. The authors discussed a novel end-to-end generative adversarial network-based method in [80]. The method explains the construction of a CNN based on adversarial training that could discriminate between segmentation maps coming either from the ground truth or generated by the segmentation model.

10. In [81], a GAN-based architecture using densely connected convolutional neural networks (DenseNets) to be able to super-resolve overhead imagery with a factor of up to 8 times is reported.

11. In [82], a method of improved generative adversarial networks (GANs) for the automatic segmentation of building footprints from satellite images. The method comprises conditional GAN (CGAN) with a cost function derived from the Wasserstein distance and which adds a gradient penalty term.

12. The authors in [83] evaluate a training methodology for pixel-wise segmentation on high-resolution satellite images using progressive growing of generative adversarial networks.

13. In [84], the authors proposed an Adversarial Saliency Detection Network (ASDN) to enhance the spatial continuity of the saliency maps with two sub-networks which are saliency detection networks and discriminator network, respectively. The discriminator aims to distinguish the saliency maps predicted by the saliency detection network from the ground truth.

14. In [85], a method for training the referring image segmentation model in a generative adversarial fashion, which well addresses the distribution similarity problem is reported.

15. In [86], a method of adversarial learning-based framework, unsupervised adversarial image retrieval (UAIR) image segmentation is reported.

Some of the Adversarial learning-based technique is discussed above. These methods are DL-based and use two networks for better reliable results. These methods describe the advantage of both supervised and unsupervised adversarial learning

1.3   Motivation

Information extraction from satellite images is a vital element of GIS systems. For extracting relevant contents from the satellite image, it is necessary to fix the RoI, perform segment/RoI identification, classification and segmentation. Of late, the approaches have been towards the use of automated methods. This is because these methods reduce human involvement and improve reliability. In such a backdrop, ML and DL-based approaches have started to receive greater attention. Our work focuses on a class of ML and DL-based approaches for content extraction of satellite images. The objective is to formulate efficient and reliable approaches of information extraction for a range of applications. Specially, we focus on the design of the ANN-based approach for image segmentation which receives RoI inputs from the K-means clustering (KCM) block. Next, a supervised approach for RoI extraction is developed which helps in performance improvement of the image segmentation approach. But the above approaches have demonstrated certain limitations in terms of the requirement of data labeling and performance bottleneck which are address using GAN-based approaches. The motivation is to explore performance improvement of a class of ML and DL-based methods configured for content extraction of satellite images.

1.4 Objective

Satellite images carry essential information required for a range of applications. Information extraction from satellite images is a challenging issue and requires a host of support. Further automation of information extraction, reliability, and decision-making regarding content is an essential and vital element. Several approaches for semantic segmentation are exits in the literature. Many of these approaches depend on the characteristics of images that can be measured. For this reason, these methods work well in some of the cases and do not work well in others. Again, there are some unintentional alterations in the images due to noise, image intensity non-uniformity, missing or occluded portion in the image etc. Therefore, for segmentation in complex images, methods based on prior knowledge may be more suitable than other approaches. For these reasons, neuro-computing methods with learning algorithms have been applied a lot in the literature [6][7][8]. Of late, among the learning-based approaches, deep neural network (DNN) supported methods have been too efficient and reliable. Therefore the objectives of the work are outlined below:

1. To derive methods for content extraction of satellite images based on prior knowledge.

2. To design a machine learning-based classifier for deriving proper class/region of satellite images.

3. To derive methods based on DL for better accuracy and efficiency.

1.5   Problem Formulation

Satellite images have been used in various applications for several decades and have made significant contributions to our understanding of the earth and human-environment inter-actions. After a detailed study considering the importance of information extraction from satellite images, we have planned to focus our work in the following three directions.

1. Segmentation of required sections from satellite images using ANN-based approach is the first attempt. A lot of characteristics that are associated with nature may be there in a satellite image such as color, shape, texture or structure, density etc. Most classification systems use the basic classification methods for low and high-resolution images. These systems give satisfactory results for low-resolution images, but with new high-resolution images, these same basic methods cannot provide satisfactory results. Problems with high resolution include the distinct presence of distortion and noise, degradations due to imperfection in the sensors and faulty calibration etc. So image extraction using conventional approaches have a significant portion of reliability overshadowed by sizable imperfections [3]. An ideal algorithm of image segmentation is expected to extract regions of satellite images that are unknown or new. Therefore,

for segmentation in complex images, methods based on learning developed using prior knowledge may be more suitable than other approaches. For these reasons neuro-computing methods with learning appropriate algorithms for content extraction of satellite Images have been considered to be beneficial.

2. The second area is the application of DNN based approach for image segmentation and identification. DL is becoming popular since it is useful for real-world applications due to the efficiency and reliability it generates. Its work is based on in-depth learning of features and mapping these to probable output state. DNNs demonstrate the ability of dynamic and automated feature learning, independence from the labeling of data, hierarchical feature map formation, and objective-driven training that takes place layer by layer and at the classification block [114]. Most of the semantic segmentation problems are performed using deep networks, such as CNNs. In terms of efficiency and accuracy, these methods are surpassing other methods extensively. Therefore, a DL-based classifier for deriving proper class/ region of satellite images is expected to be efficient for real-world applications.

3. Deep networks require substantial annotated visual data. In the case of content extraction of satellite images, the annotation should be at the pixel-level (i.e., each pixel of training images must be annotated), which is difficult to obtain. Moreover, the problem of over-fitting in deep networks will become severe if limited training data are used. For high-resolution satellite images, limited training data is a familiar problem as the collection of such images is either expensive or time demanding. An alternative to supervised learning is the unsupervised method leveraging a large amount of available unlabeled visual data. Unfortunately, unsupervised learning methods have not been very successful for semantic segmentation, because they lack the notion of classes and merely try to identify consistent regions and/or region boundaries[96]. Semi-supervised learning is halfway between supervised and unsupervised learning,

where in addition to unlabeled data, some supervision is also given, e.g., some of the samples are labeled. Generative Adversarial Networks (GAN) can be used for semantic segmentation with semi-supervised learning algorithms. This is another wide area of research considered for the work.

4. The high-resolution satellite images are often contaminated by random noise during the acquisition and transmission phase. The overall noise characteristics depend on many factors, such as sensor type, temperature, illumination, exposure time, and interference during transmission. The existence of noise not only degrades the visual quality but also restricts the subsequent processing by leading to erroneous results. Therefore, a DL-based method is expected to be beneficial to remove noise and extraction of required RoIs.

1.6   Methodology and Dataset

The methodology adopted for the study involves different steps as depicted in Fig. 1.1. At First, a detailed review of the literature related to the work done is discussed which is divided into three parts such as, ML-based, DL-based, and adversarial learning-based methods. After a detailed study considering the importance of information extraction from satellite images, we have planned to focus our work in three directions. First is the design of an ANN-based classifier to extract the RoI of satellite image where the target to the system is selected using the KMC algorithm. Second, is the implementation of a specific deep learning tool (popularly called SegNet) for image segmentation using the segmented image extracts obtained using a clustering approach. Then, semi adversarial learning-based approach, which is a combination of the segmentation network and discriminator networks as part of the Generative Adversarial Network (GAN) which is most effective in extracting content from satellite images. Finally, a Contractive Autoencoder-aided deep learning-based approach

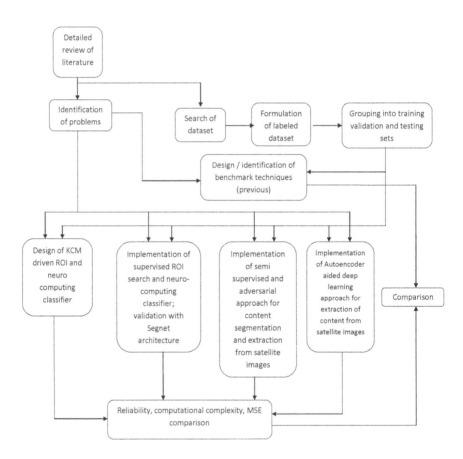

Fig. 1.1 Methodology adopted for the work

is also presented for extraction of satellite images. The four methods are compared with existing methods in terms of reliability, computational complexity and Mean Square Error (MSE).

Two datasets are used for this work. First is the United States Geological Survey [102] dataset and second is the DeepGlobe Land Cover Classification Challenge [108].

United States Geological Survey [102] dataset is a high-resolution public dataset. The total number of satellite images in the dataset is 1000 with varying sizes. The geometric resolutions of the images are 0.25 m, 0.3 m, and 0.4 m with an accuracy of 4.0 m, 5.0 m, and 3.0 m respectively. Here, resolution refers to the smallest size an object or detail can be represented in an image, and accuracy, on the other hand, is the distance between the actual geographic location of an object or detail compared to the position of the object in the image. The images cover $810km^2$ of area. The images used for the work mainly contain three classes as Sea region, House region, and Grass region.

The dataset used for the work is the DeepGlobe Land Cover Classification Challenge [108] dataset is the first public dataset of satellite images with high resolution which focuses mainly on rural areas. The total number of satellite images in the dataset is 1146 with 20448×20448 size. The dataset is divided into training, validation and test images. The numbers of training images are 803 (70% of total images), validation are 171 (15% of total images) and test images are 171 (15% of total images. The images are RGB images, with 50 cm of resolution and 7.0m of accuracy. The images cover approximately $10716.9km^2$ of the total area.

Each image in the dataset is paired with label map annotation. The label image contains 7 classes that follows the Anderson Classification [23]. The class distributions that are considered include the following:

1. Urban land: Man-made, built-up areas with human artifacts.

2. Agriculture Land (the place of cultivation done by humans, examples can be: paddy fields, farmland of plantations etc.)

3. Rangeland (grassland, all other green lands except for forest and farm)

4. Urban Land (the place of human-constructed structures)

5. Barren Land (land with no plant life, hills, rocks, mountains, desert, seashore)

6. Water (stream, waterway, reservoir, river, sea, ocean, lakes, ponds, pools, wetland)

7. Unknown region (others regions such as clouds).

1.7   Thesis Organization and Contribution

The chapter-wise contents are summarized as below-

1. **Chapter 1** gives a review of the background literature related to the work, motivation, and objective of the work including the problem identified are included in this chapter. The literature survey has been divided into three distinct parts.

2. **Chapter 2** describes the basic theoretical aspects that are related to satellite image segmentation. The theoretical considerations are important for the implementation of the proposed objective.

3. **Chapter 3** explains two approaches for content extraction of satellite images. In the first method, a simplified ANN-based approach for the segmentation of images in complex backgrounds is proposed. The work considers the formation and training of an ANN in which the pixel values of the various region of the satellite image is used as the target. Further, instead of manually selecting the RoI, a KMC based approach is adopted to help the classifier to learn/identify the sections to be extracted. The performance is found to be better than the benchmark technique reported earlier.

Yet certain limitations like the use of classical ANN restrict the performance of the approach which is addressed by a different method discussed in Chapter 3.

4. **Chapter 4** reports an approach based on deep learning for semantic segmentation of satellite images. The method comprises of training and formation of a SegNet where the input images are satellite images. In the work, the target to the network has been taken from the output of the algorithm of KCM with their label of the required region of interest (RoI). The RoI is reinforced by the learning of the CNN which is later used for extraction and identification. Then, with the output of the SegNet as input and the pixel values of various RoI as the target, a neuro-computing structure is trained as a classifier to segment the various RoIs. The performance is found to be better than that obtained from the work reported in Chapter 3.

5. In **Chapter 5** a semi-supervised adversarial learning method is reported which is used for content extraction from satellite images. Two learning-based networks are used. The first is a segmentation network that uses unlabeled data and supervised learning. Next, a discriminator network which is a CNN and used to improve the segmentation accuracy. The outputs of the segmentation network are used as input to the classifier to extract the region of interest (RoIs) of the satellite image and reinforce the decision. This approach provides the best outcome.

6. **Chapter 6** describes a deep learning-based method to extract different regions of interest(RoIs)is presented in which a DL-based noise removal process from the input high-resolution satellite images is also included. In the work, at first, the high-resolution satellite images are processed with the Contractive Autoencoder (CAE) to remove the noise which is inherently present in the images during acquisition. The output of the CAE is taken as input to train a segmentation network which is a deep neural network. Finally, the output of the segmentation network is used to train both supervised and

unsupervised classifiers to extract different RoIs from the satellite images. The results obtained are reliable and efficient in terms of accuracy.

7. **Chapter 7** concludes the thesis. It summarizes the present research work. Findings of the present work, limitation of the present work, and scope for fur the improvements are described in the chapter.

The specific contributions of the work are-

1. Formulation of an ANN-based approach for segmentation of satellite images in the complex background where, by selecting the RoIs, using manual and KCM approaches the classifier can segment the particular region out of the satellite image.

2. The use of a semi-supervised method for extraction of RoIs in satellite images for image segmentation using deep architecture is another contribution. It reduces the complexities encountered in obtaining the annotated data for satellite images.

3. Using of SegNet in the method of Chapter 4 in the combination of supervised approach trained extensively using sizable data increases the accuracy in terms of MSE and mean intersection over union (IOU).

4. The combination of semi-supervised training adversarial learning algorithm increases the effectiveness and accuracy of the content extraction of satellite images. The use of segmentation and discriminator networks improves the performance considerably.

5. A Contractive Autoencoder aided deep learning-based approach to deals with the problem of high-resolution satellite images which may contain noise during acquisition that affect the performance of the segmentation process.

1.8 Conclusion

In this chapter, a review of the background is included. Literature related to the work, motivation, and objective of the work including problems identified are included in this chapter. The description of the basic theoretical aspects that are related to satellite image segmentation and the theoretical considerations that are important for the implementation of the proposed objective is included in the second chapter. The subsequent chapters comprise the experimental works and the results derived.

2

Theoretical Consideration

In this chapter, the basic theoretical considerations related to satellite image segmentation and learning-based techniques that help in better understanding the process related to information extraction from satellite images are reported. Further, basic approaches of image segmentation used in the work are also included. Again some of the factors for quality measurement used to describe the performance of the methods are included in the chapter.

2.1   Satellite Image Segmentation

Remote sensing is an important technology to study various parts of the Earth. Most of the satellite images are ill-defined or not clear for many reasons. Therefore, there may be difficulty in recognizing the important information embedded in the images. The widespread information contained in a satellite image can be improved by image enhancement techniques, but cannot be detectable. These techniques are used to enhance the picture quality to acquire useful information. There are several techniques that have been developed for the enhancement of the quality of satellite images [87]. In ML, image segmentation is a topic where one needs to categorize the image on a per-pixel level. Here, the satellite image should be represented by a map where each region in the image is automatically categorized, just like generating a map view automatically from satellite images.

Earlier many methods for satellite image segmentation have been developed. J.Yang et al. [88] proposed an unsupervised multi-band approach for scale parameter selection in the multi-scale image segmentation process, which uses spectral angle to measure the spectral homogeneity of segments. J. Liu et.al. [89] proposed a novel image segmentation method for very-high-resolution (VHR) multispectral images using combined spectral and morphological information. Z. Huang et al. [90] has proposed the novel feature for remote sensing image analysis, called multi-scale relative salience (MsRS) feature. It was constructed by modeling the process of feature value changing with scales. Z. Wang et al. [91]] introduced a new automatic region-based image segmentation algorithm based on k-means clustering (RISA), specifically designed for remote sensing applications.

Now a days, many deep learning-based satellite image segmentation have been developed which are more reliable in terms of accuracy. H. Xie et al. [92] first introduce multi-layer feature learning for polarimetric synthetic aperture radar (PolSAR) classification, where Stacked Autoencoder (SAE) is employed to extract useful features from a channel PolSAR image. J. Geng et al. [93] propose a deep convolutional autoencoder (DCAE) to extract features and conduct classification automatically. J. Geng et al. [94] later propose a similar framework, called deep supervised and contractive neural network (DSCNN), for SAR image classification.

Over the years certain classes of techniques have been reported. For the present work, such methods are grouped into statistical and learning-based methods. Further, learning-based methods may be ML or DL-based. ML methods represent early generation ANN and certain overlap DL-based approaches. DL methods revolve around approaches which demonstrate programmable feature learning and extraction hierarchy, use of unlabeled data, supervised or unsupervised or a mixture of both learning approach.

2.1.1   Statistical/spatial or non- learning based methods

The process of partitioning an image into multiple segments is called image segmentation. The goal of image segmentation is to obtain a representation of an image with distinct partitions of common content with something meaningful. The representation should enable subsequent analysis. It is typically used to locate objects and boundaries in images. There are many approaches to segment an image such as intensity-based methods, discontinuity-based methods, similarity-based methods, clustering methods, graph-based methods, Pixon-based methods, hybrid methods [15] etc. Most of these methods rely on the image characteristics they are measuring. Therefore, they work well in certain cases and not in others. For example, edge detection-based image segmentation methods do not work well for images with ill-defined edges. Similarly, thresholding-based methods do not work well with images without any obvious peaks or with a broad layout and at valleys. Though the above approaches have been found to be reliable, these have certain limitations are required human intervention. Moreover, the images are usually corrupted by several artifacts, such as image noise, missing or occluded parts, image intensity inhomogeneity or non-uniformity. Therefore, when

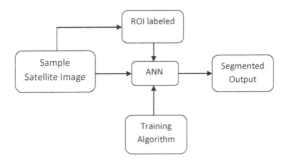

Fig. 2.1 ANN based image segmentation.

dealing with complex images, some prior knowledge may be necessary to disambiguate the segmentation process.

2.2   Machine Learning Techniques

A generic ANN based image segmentation block diagram is shown in Fig. 2.1.

Several learning-based methods for segmentation have been developed until now. An ANN architecture had been developed for the region of interest (RoI) segmentation of fingerprint images in [14] where the authors trained ANNs with 10000 samples extracted from 20 fingerprint images. S. Arumugadevi et.al. in [15], proposed a method in which supervised feed-forward neural network are trained where the labels obtained from the clustering method FCM are used as a target . In [16], Backpropagation ANN was used to get iterative calculations of image pixel for image segmentation. An unsupervised, non-parametric method using Variable Structure Self Organizing MAP (VSSOM) and Parameterless Self Organizing MAP (PLSOM) is reported in [27]. P. Upadhyay et. al. [18] also proposed a method using Modified Self Organizing Feature Map (SOFM) ANN. They modified the SOFM ANN by adding an extra layer of neurons. C. Wang et.al. [19] developed a method an image segmentation method based on Pulse Coupled Neural Network (PCNN) and Independent Component Analysis (ICA). The authors in [20] also developed a method for segmentation using PCNN where they combined 1-dimensional Maximal Correlative Criterion with 2-dimensional Maximal Correlative Criterion to estimate neuron parameters.

ANNs had also been used in medical image segmentation. In [21], ANN based segmentation method for a lesion in brain MRI where training was done using gray levels and extracted statistical features from the training data with the labeled ground truth. M. J. Moghaddam et.al. [22] had developed a method of segmentation where deep brain structures were segmented using Geometric Moment Invariants (GMIs) and MLP ANNs. In [23], a method for leukocyte image segmentation had been developed where feed-forward ANN with random weights is employed to classify all the pixels in a leukocyte image. Then, according to the classification results, the regions of the nucleus and cytoplasm are extracted, respectively, to achieve the segmentation.

ANN is a mathematical or computational model inspired by biological neural networks. It consists of an interconnected group of artificial neurons and processes information using a connectionist approach to computation. The ANN in a feed-forward form called MLP is conFig.d to learn applied patterns. The process of learning patterns by an ANN is called training. MLPs are trained using (error) Back Propagation (BP) depending upon which the connecting weights between the layers are updated. This adaptive updating of the MLP is continued till the performance goal is met [103]. The steps are as below,

Initialization: Initialize weight matrix W with random values between $[0, 1]$.

The training samples: The input is $I_p = [i_{p1}, i_{p2}, \ldots i_{pn}]$. The desired output is, $T_p = [t_{p1}, t_{p2}, \ldots t_{pn}]$. The hidden nodes are computed as follows,

$$N_{pq}^q = \Sigma_{x=1}^n \omega_{yx}^q I^{px} + \Phi_y^q \tag{2.1}$$

The output from the hidden layer are calculated as-

$$O_{py}^q = f_y^q(N_{py}^q) \tag{2.2}$$

Where $f(X)$ depends upon the choice of activation function.

The values of the output nodes are calculated as-

$$O_{pl}^r = f_l^r(N_{py}^r) \tag{2.3}$$

Computation of errors: The errors are computed as-

$$E_{ye} = T_{ye} - O_{ye} \tag{2.4}$$

The mean square error (MSE) is calculated as-

$$MSE = \frac{\sum_{y=1}^{N} \sum_{e=1}^{n} E_{ye}^2}{2N} \tag{2.5}$$

The errors for the output layer is calculated as follows-

$$\delta_{pm}^r = O_{pm}^r(1 - O_{pm}^r)E_{pe} \tag{2.6}$$

The errors for the hidden layer is calculated as-

$$\delta_{pm}^q = O_{pm}^q(1 - O_{pm}^q)\sum_y \delta_{py}^r \omega_{ym} \tag{2.7}$$

Weight Update: The weights between the output and hidden layers are updated as-

$$\omega_{my}^r(t+1) = \omega_{my}^r(t) + \eta \delta_{pm}^r O_{py} \tag{2.8}$$

Where η is the learning rate $(0 < \eta < 1)$. The weights between the hidden and input layers are updated as-

$$\omega_{yx}^{q}(t+1) = \omega_{yx}^{q}(t) + \eta \, \delta_{py}^{q} I_x \tag{2.9}$$

One cycle through the complete training set forms one epoch. The above is repeated till MSE meets the performance criteria. At first, the MLP is trained with one hidden layer and then it is trained with two and three hidden layers. The input and output layers use log-sigmoid activation while the hidden layers use tan-sigmoid activation functions. In the subsequent section of the work, the following classes of BP algorithms have been used.

1. **Levenberg- Marquardt Back-propagation (LMBP):** LMBP has been designed to work specifically with loss functions which take the form of a sum of squared errors.

2. **Scaled Conjugate Gradient (SCG):** In SCG the search is performed along with conjugate directions which produces generally faster convergence.

3. **Conjugate Gradient back-propagation with polak-ribiere updates (CGBP):** CGBP is a network training function that updates weight and bias values according to conjugate gradient backpropagation with Polak-Ribiere updates.

4. **Bayesian Regulation back-propagation (BRBP):** BRBP is a network training function that updates the weight and bias values according to Levenberg-Marquardt optimization. It minimizes a combination of squared errors and weights and then determines the correct combination so as to produce a network that generalizes well. The process is called Bayesian regularization.

5. **Resilient back-propagation (RBP):** is a network training function that updates weight and bias values according to the resilient BP algorithm.

2.3 Deep Learning Techniques

Deep learning (DL) is a type of ML and artificial intelligence (AI) that imitates the way humans gain certain types of knowledge. DL is an important element that includes statistics and predictive modeling. It is extremely beneficial to one whose tasked with collecting, analyzing and interpreting large amounts of data. DL makes the process easier and accurate. Various methods have been developed for image segmentation with CNN (a common deep learning architecture), which have become indispensable in tackling more advanced challenges with image segmentation. Basically, segmentation is a process that partitions an image into regions. It is an image processing approach that allows us to separate objects and textures in images.

Presently, DL is becoming popular since it is very useful for real-world applications due to the efficiency and reliability it generates. Deep learning algorithms have solved several computer vision tasks with an increasing level of difficulty. Its working is based on in-depth learning of features and mapping these to probable output state. Most of the semantic segmentation problems are performed using deep networks, such as CNNs [9][10][11]. In terms of efficiency and accuracy, these methods are surpassing other methods extensively.

During the last decades, learning aided or AI-based approaches have been adopted for satellite image analysis and information extraction. Lately, the shift has been towards the use of deep learning which is now the omnipresent approach for the development of learning aided or AI-based techniques. Many deep learning-based methods and architecture for image segmentation are available in the literature which adopts prior knowledge as a means of information extraction and content retrieval in computer vision domains. AlexNet [10], VGG-16 [114], ResNet [115], RCNN [116] etc. are such architectures which achieved significant achievements in image semantic segmentation. Most of the other state-of-the-art algorithms are based on these approaches. A few DNN types used for the work are SegNet and GAN. These are discussed below.

SegNet

It is a deep fully convolutional neural network [8]. The architecture was developed for semantic pixel-wise segmentation. It has an encoder network. The encoder network is followed by a corresponding decoder network. Then a final pixel-wise classification layer follows the network. The layers in the encoder and decoder network are explained below:

1. **Convolutional layer:** Convolutional layer is a bank of simple filters. It has learnable parameters. Let us consider the size of the input layer X be $W_1 \times H_1 \times D_1$. This layer convolves with the filter bank. Here the stride is S and padding P units. Then the result of the operation will be an output Y whose size will be $W_2 \times H_2 \times D_2$ as shown in Fig.2.2. The output at spatial position (i,j) of Y formulates as:

$$Y_{ij} = \omega \times N_{ij} + b \tag{2.10}$$

where b and ω are the bias and weights respectively which are learnable parameters of the layer, N_{ij} is the corresponding receptive field. The dimension of the spatial output of the layer are given by $W_2 = (W_1 - F + 2P)/S + 1$, $H_2 = (H_1 - F + 2P)/S + 1$. Here F is the size of the receptive field or spatial size of the filters. In this work, the convolution filters are of size 3×3. The output volume neuron size is $F \times F \times D_1$. By the method of parameter sharing the learnable weights and bias of Y are shared across the spatial location of X.

2. **Non-Linear Function Layer:** A non-linear function layer is situated after the convolution layer. This layer is called an activation function. The Activation function introduces non-linearity in the network. The rectified linear unit (ReLU) function [95], $f(x) = \max(0, x)$, is the activation function which is most commonly used.

3. **Pooling Layer:** Using the MAX operation, the Pooling Layer resizes every depth slice of the input spatially and independently. The filters of size 2×2 with a stride of 2 is

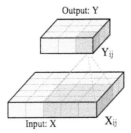

Fig. 2.2 Illustration of convolutional layer: Convolution performed using input of size $W1 \times H1 = 5 \times 5$, with filter size (receptive field, F) 3, stride S=2 and padding P=0. The output Y will be of size 3×3.

the most common form of a pooling layer. Along both width and height, the pooling layer discard 75% of ReLU layer output by downsampling by 2. The depth dimension will not changed. The pooling layer output will be $W_2 = (W_1 - F)/S + 1$, $H_2 = (H_1 - F)/S + 1$, $D_2 = D_1$. Here the input volume is of size $W_1 \times H_1 \times D_1$. F is filter size and S is the Stride.

4. **Unpooling layer:** The locations of the maxima in the output of each pooling area are recorded in the unpooling operation. In the deconvolution, by preserving the structure of the stimulus, the unpooling operation places the values from the layer of pooling into appropriate locations, using these recorded locations.

5. **Deconvolution layer:** The deconvolution layer, also known as the transposed layer, is shown in Fig. 2.3. For upsampling operation this layer is commonly used. The input to the layer is first up-sampled with stride S and padding P. Then, with a filter bank, convolution is performed in the input to up-sampled it with the receptive field of size F. It is inverse of convolution. The parameters of the filter can be set to be learned.

6. **Softmax classifier:** Softmax layer also referred to as a normalized exponential function. It squashes a k-dimensional vector(z) to a k- dimensional vector $(\sigma(z))$ in the

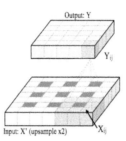

Fig. 2.3 Illustration of deconvolutional layer: deconvolution performed using input of size $W1 \times H1 = 3 \times 3$, with filter size (receptive field, F) 3, stride S=2 and padding P=1. The output Y will be of size 5×5 [95].

range $(0,1)$ that add up to 1. The equation is as follows-

$$\sigma = \Re^k \rightarrow (0,1)^k \qquad (2.11)$$

$$\sigma(z)_j = \frac{e^{z_j}}{\sum_{k=1}^{k} e^{z_k}} \qquad (2.12)$$

The Softmax classifier uses the cross-entropy loss. Each pixel is examined by this loss individually, comparing the class predictions to the target.

In SegNet, with a filter blank each encoder performs convolution. This produces a set of feature maps. The feature maps are then batch normalized. An element-wise ReLU, $(\max(0,x))$ is performed after batch normalization. Following that, max-pooling with a non-overlapping window with stride 2 is performed. The window is of size 2×2. Then the output of max-pooling is sub-sampled by 2. The max-pooling indices are stored and used in the decoder network. Using the stored max-pooling indices, the decoder network upsamples the input feature maps. This step produces sparse feature maps. To produce dense feature maps the feature maps are convolved with a trainable decoder filter bank. Finally, a trainable soft-max classifier is used to process the high-dimensional feature representation of the final decoder output. Each pixel is classified by this soft-max classifier independently. The resultant segmentation is the class with maximum probability at each pixel [8].

Using the RoI as input and the label image of each RoI as the target, the SegNet is trained with Stochastic Gradient Decent (SGD) using BP as a gradient computing technique. This method is adopted here since the weight update technique has the ability to train end to end to jointly optimize the network weights.

The algorithm for training the SegNet is given below. In algorithm 1 and algorithm 2 training of encoder and decoder are described and in algorithm 3 batch normalization is presented [96].

Algorithm 1 Training an encoder: Training start with a input image of size $X1 \times H1 \times D1$. The size of the output is $X2 \times H2 \times D2$. Here, the cost function for mini-batch is denoted by C. The value λ denotes the learning rate decay factor and L denotes the numbers of layers. the batch-normalize activations are denoted by *BatchNorm()*. The *ReLU()* performs activation $(\max(0,x))$ of the given input. The *Conv()* performs operations of convolution with a filter size = 3, S = 1(stride) and P = 1(zero padding). The pooling operation is performed by The *Pool()* with Max pooling filter with kernel size = 2, S = 2(stride) and P = 0(zero padding).

Require: A mini-batch of inputs and targets (p,t), previous weights W, previous Batch Normalization parameters θ, weights initialization coefficients from γ, and previous learning rate η.

Ensure: Weights updating $W^t + 1$, Batch-Normalization parameters updating θ^{t+1} and learning rate updating η^{t+1}.

- **Step1:** Input $X1 \times H1 \times D1$ size image.

- **Step2:** for k = 0 to L-1

  Repeat:

    1. $W_{bk} \leftarrow BN(W_k)$

    2. $W_{rk} \leftarrow ReLU(W_k)$

    3. $W_{ck} \leftarrow Conv.(W_{rk}, W_{bk})$

    4. $Pl_{kmask}, Pl_k \leftarrow Pool(W_{ck})$

    5. **if** $k \leq L$ **then**

        $W_k \leftarrow Pl_k$

        return Pl_{kmask}

- **Step3:** Stop

Algorithm 2. Decoder training: Input pooling mask size is of $X_2 \times H_2 \times D_2$. The output is of size $X_D \times H_D \times D_D$. Here, the cost function for mini-batch is denoted by C. The value λ denotes the learning rate decay factor and L denotes the numbers of layers. The function that up-samples the given inputs is denoted by $Upsample()$. As the encoder configurations, The $ReLU()$ and $Conv()$ will perform the same operations. To output the class probabilities $SoftMax()$ is used which is a multi-class softmax classifier.

Require: A mini-batch of feature maps extracted from encoder network of size $X_2 \times H_2 \times D_2$. Previous weights W, previous Batch Normalization parameters θ, weights initialization coefficients from γ, and previous learning rate η.

Ensure: Weights updating W^{t+1}, Batch-Normalization parameters updating θ^{t+1} and learning rate updating η^{t+1}.

- Step1: Input Pl_{kmask}, Pl_k

- Step2: for k = L to 1

Repeat:

    1. $F_{dk} \leftarrow Upsample(Pl_{kmask}, Pl_k)$

    2. $F_{dbk} \leftarrow BatchNorm(F_{dk})$

3. $F_{dek} \leftarrow ReLU(F_{dk})$

4. $F_{dck} \leftarrow Conv(F_{dek}, F_{dbk})$

5. **if** $k > 1$ **then**

    $P_{lk} \leftarrow F_{dck}$

    else return

    $SoftMax(F_{dck})$

- Stop.

Algorithm3. Batch normalization [96]: Let us consider the normalized values and their corresponding linear transformations be be $\hat{x}_{1...m}$ and $y_{1...m}$ respectively. $BN_{\gamma,\beta} : x_{1...m} \rightarrow y_{1...m}$. refers the transformation. For numerical stability The value ε is added, which is a constant, to the mini-batch variance.

Require: Values of x over a mini-batch: $B = x_{1...m}$; Parameters to be learned: γ, β

Ensure: $y_i = BN(x_i, \gamma, \beta)$

$\mu_B \leftarrow \frac{1}{m}\sum_{i=1}^{m} x_i$ //mini-batch mean

$\sigma_B^2 \leftarrow \frac{1}{m}\sum_{i=1}^{m}(x_i - \mu_B)^2$ //mini-batch variance

$\hat{x}_i \leftarrow \frac{x_i - \mu_B}{\sqrt{\sigma_B^2 + \varepsilon}}$ //normalize

$y_i \leftarrow \gamma\hat{x}_i + \beta = BN(x_i, \gamma, \beta)$ //scale and shift

Generative Adversarial Network (GAN)

A class of powerful neural networks called GANs [13] is used for unsupervised learning. GANs are consist of a system of two neural network models which compete with each other. The two parts are called Generator and Discriminator. They are trained in an adversarial manner. The main objective of G is to generate samples as the target data as real as possible. D will attempt to differentiate the generated samples from the target ones. Since the two

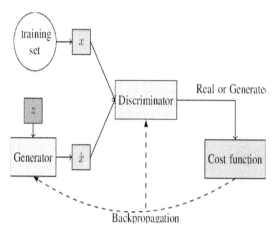

Fig. 2.4 Generative Adversarial Network

networks are trained through back-propagation, therefore the G and D will be better in their respective jobs after each training cycle. The working can be seen by the Fig. 2.4:

Here, the generator takes in a random image and returns an image. This generated image is fed into the discriminator alongside a stream of images taken from the actual, ground-truth dataset. The discriminator takes in both real and fake images and returns probabilities, a number between 0 and 1, with 1 representing a prediction of authenticity and 0 representing fake. The discriminator network is trained by minimizing the spatial cross-entropy loss,

$$D_l = -\sum_{m,n}(1-x_n)\log(1-Q(P(X_n))^{(m,n)} + x_n\log(Q(\widehat{X}_n)^{(m,n)}) \qquad (2.13)$$

Here, $x_n = 0$, if the input from the discriminator network is from the generator and $x_n = 1$ if it is from the ground truth. $Q(P(X_n)^{(}m,n)$ is the output of discriminator at location (m,n), when input to the discriminator is X_n and $Q(\widehat{X}_n)^{(m,n)}$ is its output at location (m,n), when input to the discriminator is $\widehat{X}_n$.

Contractive Autoencoder

A contractive autoencoder [100]is an unsupervised deep learning technique that helps a neural network encode unlabeled training data. The contractive autoencoder (CAE) objective is to have a robust learned representation that is less sensitive to the small variation in the data. The robustness of the representation for the data is done by applying a penalty term to the loss function. The penalty term is the Frobenius norm of the Jacobian matrix. The Frobenius norm of the Jacobian matrix for the hidden layer is calculated with respect to the input.

Here, the input, I, is encoded by the CAE using function g, and to make the output identical to the input, the encoded values $g(I)$ are decoded with a function h. As the objective of the CAE is to obtain a vigorous representation of the learned pattern, therefore, to make the output less sensitive to the small variations in the input, a penalty term, Frobenius norm of the Jacobian matrix (J_f) added to the loss function of the CAE. J_f is the sum of the square of all the elements and it is calculated with respect to the inputs for the hidden layers. Therefore, the loss function of the CAE is given by,

$$l = |I - h(g(I)| + \lambda \|J_F(I)\|_F^2 \qquad (2.14)$$

$$\|J_F(I)\|_F^2 = \sum_{i,j} (\frac{\partial h_j(I)}{\partial I_i})^2 \qquad (2.15)$$

where, λ is the coefficient of weight decay which controls the relative importance of regularization. CAE is a better choice than denoising autoencoder to learn useful feature extraction. Fig. 2.5 shows the structure of CAE.

Deeplab-v2

The DeepLab series published four iterations called V1, V2, V3, and V3+. DeepLab V1 sets the foundation of this series, V2, V3, and V3+ each brings some improvement over the

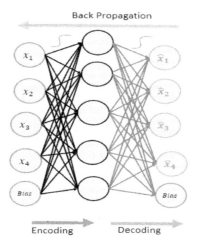

Fig. 2.5 Structure of Contractive Autoencoder (CAE) [100]

previous version. These four iterations borrowed innovations from image classification in recent years to improve semantic segmentation and also inspired lots of other research works in this area. The figure, Fig.2.6 is the DeepLab-v2 model architecture. First, the input image goes through the network with the use of atrous convolution and Atrous Spatial Pyramid Pooling. Then the output from the network is bilinearly interpolated and goes through the fully connected CRF to fine-tune the result and get the final output [122].

2.4 Basic Approaches

In this work, we have adopted KCM and FCM clustering to fix the RoI. and Quality measurement factors. Some of the measuring quality include MSE, Accuracy, Confusion matrix, mean IOU, Structural similarity index (SSI) etc. The basic notions related to the work are discussed here.

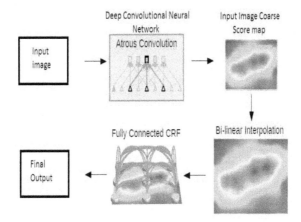

Fig. 2.6 Architecture of Deeplab-v2 model [122]

2.4.1   K-means (KMC) clustering

The aim of clustering analysis is to group data in such a way that similar objects are in one cluster and dissimilar objects are in different clusters. K-means clustering (KCM) algorithm is an algorithm to classify or group the objects K groups. K is a positive integer number. The grouping is done by minimizing the Euclidean distances between data and the corresponding cluster centroid. The steps of the algorithm are as follows:

Let us consider the image that is to be cluster is of resolution of $x \times y$. Let the input pixel to be cluster be $p(x,y)$ and the cluster centers be c_k. The KCM algorithm is following as[97][98]:

1. The cluster number k, and their center be initialized.

2. The Euclidean distance d, between the initialized center and each image pixel, be calculated as-

$$d = \|p(x,y) - c_k\| \qquad (2.16)$$

3. Based on distance d, to the nearest centers, all pixels in the image be assigned.

4. New position of the center be recalculated after assigning all pixels using the relation given below.

$$c_k = \frac{1}{k} \sum_{y \varepsilon c_k} \sum_{x \varepsilon c_k} p(x, y) \tag{2.17}$$

5. The process be repeated until it achieved minimum error value.

6. Then the pixels in the cluster be reshaped into the image.

The index returned by the algorithm corresponds to the clusters in the image. Using these index values labeling every pixel in the image is done.

2.4.2 Fuzzy C-means (FCM) clustering

One of the common and popular algorithms that are used for image segmentation is the (FCM) algorithm. In this algorithm, the image is divided into various cluster regions and each cluster contains similar values of the pixel of the image. It is a suitable clustering method for satellite image segmentation. The FCM algorithm is a fuzzified version of the KCMA algorithm. FCM clustering technique is intended to find meaningful clusters present in a dataset by assigning some membership values in the range of [0, 1]. It is a form of clustering in which each data point can belong to more than one cluster. In this method, data points are assigned to clusters in such a way that the items in the same cluster are as similar as possible, while items belonging to different clusters are as dissimilar as possible. Clusters are identified via similarity measures. These similarity measures include distance, connectivity, and intensity. Different similarity measures may be chosen based on the data or the application [98][99]. Following are steps of fuzzy c-mean clustering:

1. At least 2 random centroids be chosen and data values be included to them randomly.

2. The membership matrix be computed as:

$$U_{i,j} = \cfrac{1}{\sum_{k=1}^{c} [\frac{|x_i - c_j|}{x_i - c_k}]^{\frac{2}{m-1}}}$$

(2.18)

where $m > 1$ and c is the number of cluster.

3. The clusters centers be calculated as:

$$C = \frac{\sum_i^n U_{ij}^m \times x_i}{\sum_i^n U_{ij}^m}$$

(2.19)

4. if $C_{(k-1)} - Ck < \varepsilon$ then Stop else go to Step2. Here,ε is the termination criterion between [0, 1].

Since it is an iterative algorithm as it computes membership value for each item in the data. Therefore the algorithm consumes more time and memory.

2.4.3   Quality measurements

Some of the quality measurements [113] relevant for the work are discussed below:

a. Accuracy: Accuracy indicates the percentage of correctly identified pixels in the image. The accuracy is commonly reported for each class separately as well as globally across all classes. Therefore,

$$Accuracy = \frac{TP + TN}{(TP + TN + FP + FN)}$$

(2.20)

Here, TP, TN, FP, and FN are the number of true positive, the number of true negative, the number of false positive, and the number of false-negative respectively. [113].

b. Intersection over Union (IOU): For each class, the ratio of correctly classified pixels to the total number of ground truth and predicted pixels in that class is called the IOU [113]. For images with more than one class, the mean IOU of the image is calculated by taking an average of the IOU of each class. the mean IOU is more stringent for the smaller representation of the class as it is not as affected by the class imbalances that are inherent in foreground/background segmentation tasks. Therefore,

$$IOU = \frac{TP}{(TP+FP+FN)} \tag{2.21}$$

Here, TP, FP, and FN are the number of true positive, number of false positive, and number of false-negative respectively.

c. Boundary F1-score: The boundary F1 (BF) contour matching score indicates how well the predicted boundary of each class aligns with the true boundary. It is given by the harmonic mean of precision and sensitivity or recall values [113]. Therefore,

$$F1-score = \frac{2 \times precision \times recall}{(recall + precision)} \tag{2.22}$$

Here, Precision is the ratio of the number of points on the boundary of the predicted segmentation that is close enough to the boundary of the ground truth segmentation to the length of the predicted boundary [113]. Therefore,

$$Precision = \frac{TP}{TP+FP} \tag{2.23}$$

And, Recall is the ratio of the number of points on the boundary of the ground truth segmentation that is close enough to the boundary of the predicted segmentation to the length of the ground truth boundary [113]. Therefore,

$$Recall = \frac{TP}{TP+FN} \qquad (2.24)$$

Here, TP, FP, and FN are the number of true positive, number of false positive, and number of false-negative respectively.

d. Mean Square Error (MSE): MSE is a procedure for estimating an unobserved quantity. It measures the average of the squares of the errors i.e. the average squared difference between the estimated values and the actual value. The MSE is calculated as-

$$MSE = \frac{\sum_{y=1}^{N} \sum_{e=1}^{n} E_{ye}^2}{2N} \qquad (2.25)$$

e. Structural Similarity Index (SSIM): SSIM is is used for measuring the similarity between two images. It is calculated on various windows or masks of an image. If x and y are two windows of two images of size $N \times N$, then SSIM is calculated as:

$$SSIM_{x,y} = \frac{(2\mu_x\mu_y+c_1)(2\sigma_{xy}+c_2)}{(\mu_x^2+\mu_y^2+c_3)(\sigma_x^2+\sigma_y^2+c_2)} \qquad (2.26)$$

where, $\mu_x and \mu_y$ are average of x and y respectively, σ_x and σ_x are the variance of x and y respectively, σ_{xy} is the co-variance of x and y and c_1 and c_2 are the two variables to stabilize the division with weak denominator.

f. Confusion Matrix: Confusion matrix is a square matrix, the rows of which represents the actual class of the task and columns of the matrix represents the predicted class. The confusion matrix gives the raw information about the prediction done by the model on a given dataset. All the measure of the prediction performance are based on four indices namely-

- True Positive (TP)- represents the number of correctly recognized class.

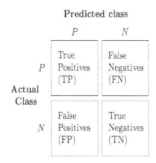

Fig. 2.7 Example of a confusion matrix

- False Positive (FP)- represents the number of examples assigned incorrectly to the class.

- True Negative (TN)- represents the number of correctly recognized examples that do not belong to the true class.

- False Negative (FN)- represents the examples that are not recognized as class examples.

A confusion matrix is shown in Fig. 2.5.

2.5   Conclusion

In this chapter, we have included the description of the basic theoretical aspects that are related to satellite image segmentation. The theoretical considerations are important for the implementation of the work. From the literature, it has been seen that ML and DL methods are extensively used for knowledge-based image segmentation.

3

Learning Aided Structures for Satellite

Image Segmentation

In this chapter, two approaches for content extraction Satellite images are reported. The first work is a feed-forward ANN-based work that requires just a few points from the RoI to capture the details of the sub-region and subsequently carry out the segmentation with any manual intervention. The second work is also a feed-forward ANN-based work, where the RoI to capture the details of the sub-region is selected using KMC. From the experimental results, both the work provides satisfactory results.[1]

---

[1] A part of this work is reported in

3.1 Introduction

The information carried by satellite images are required in a large number of applications. Extraction of these information from satellite images is a challenging task and the support required is enormous. Further, reliability, decision making, and automation regarding the contents and information extraction from these images are vital and essential elements. Therefore, efforts have been made continuously for the development of techniques and approaches to improve the accuracy of information extraction processes. Image segmentation is the frequently used approach for the extraction of different regions from satellite images. It is a process of dividing an image into meaningful multiple segments. The primary objective of image segmentation is to obtain a meaningful representation with the proper division of common objects in the image. The representation should enable subsequent analysis. The approaches based on intensity, discontinuity, similarity, clustering, hybrid methods [15] etc (as already discussed in Chapter 2) deals with the process of image segmentation. However, these methods mainly depend on some of the characteristics of the image that they are measuring. Further, while one attribute, for example, intensity, is considered, the others are disregarded. As a result, the output obtained fails to give an in-depth representation of the content assimilating all the above-mentioned attributes. All these attributes are essential for a complete description of the image content. Hence, disregarding remaining and selecting one of them shall highlight the contribution of one attribute only while neglecting the other contributions which are not a viable solution. Therefore, these may not work well in all situations. For example, in an image where the edges are not well defined, the image segmentation methods based on edge detection do not work well. Similarly, the methods

1. M. Barthakur, K. K. Sarma and N. Mastorakis, Learning Aided Structures for Image Segmentation in Complex Background, IEEE European Conference on Electrical Engineering and Computer Science (EECS 2017), Bern, Switzerland, Nov., 2017.

2. M. Barthakur, K. K. Sarma and N. Mastorakis, Neural Network methods for Image Segmentation, In Applied Physics, System Science and Computers II. APSAC 2017. Lecture Notes in Electrical Engineering, vol. 489. Springer, Cham, 2019.

based on thresholding do not work well with images with the broad layout or at valleys or without any obvious edges that might not provide the relevant details. Again, the images may be corrupted by several artifacts, such as image noise, missing or occluded parts, image intensity inhomogeneity, or non-uniformity. Therefore, when dealing with complex images, some prior knowledge may be necessary to disambiguate the segmentation process. For that purpose, learning-based and neuro-computing structures have been used extensively [15][17][101].

In this work, two approaches for content extraction of satellite images are presented. In the first method, a simplified ANN-based approach for the segmentation of images in complex backgrounds is proposed. The work considers the formation and training an ANN in which the pixel values of the various region of the satellite image is used as the target. The method does not require any feature extraction, labeling of objects, region growing or splitting methods as pre-processing steps of input to configure and train an ANN, which for the work is a multi-layer perceptron (MLP) trained with (error) BP learning. As this method require manual intervention to select the various region of the image, a second method is proposed, where KCM algorithm is used to label the particular RoI in the image, and the region is used as the target to train the MLP.

We have used the dataset (as discussed in Chapter 1), trained the MLPs with five different raining methods (LMBP, SCG, CGBP, BRBP, and RBP), used one, two, and three hidden layer configurations, and considered multi-segment classifications with special focus on the extraction of three segments with complex backgrounds. Results obtained show that two hidden layered MLP trained with the LMBP method is the best combination for the work reported here.

The subsequent description is categorized into several sections. In Section 3.2, the formulation of the neuro- computing structures is discussed in detail. The second part of the work involving MLP with RoI identification using KMC is discussed in Section 3.3.

3.2   Neuro- Computing Structures for Segmentation in Complex Background

In this work, a simplified neuro-computing structure in feed-forward form for use in the segmentation of high-resolution satellite images in complex backgrounds is proposed. The work considers the formation and training of a neuro-computing structure in which the pixel values of the various region of the image are used as the target. The method does not require any feature extraction, labeling of objects, region growing, or splitting methods to configure and train a neuro-computing structure. Here, we use an MLP trained with (error) BP learning. The neuro-computing structure is trained with different training functions. The network is also trained with single, double, and triple hidden layers. Then the MSE between the output image and desired image and the time required for training has been calculated.

3.2.1   System model

The working of the system has broad processes. First, the system is trained with image segments which are to be extracted out of the satellite feeds. The training is done extensively with a configuration of the MLP fixed with several rounds of trial and error. The MLP configuration experimented which involves one, two, and three hidden layer formats. This step is essential to know the dependence of learning that takes place with variation in the middle section of the MLP. It is found that with the addition of more hidden layers, the learning improves but an optimal state is essential for the use in the experimental part. For this aspect, MSE and accuracy have been considered to be essential parameters to select the optimal configuration. Further, BP involves several types of gradient descent approaches. We have considered five different variations of the BP training. The results obtained are discussed in Subsection 3.2.2. The combination of MLP with optimal middle section trained with the most suitable BP training forms the basis of the system. After the training is over, a

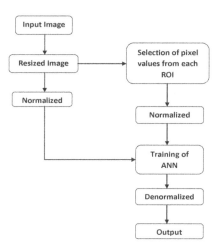

Fig. 3.1 System model of the method

few validation checks are carried out to ensure that the learning is optimal and to ascertain that over/ under training has not taken place. Finally, testing is carried out.

The block diagram for the work is shown in Fig. 3.1. The sub-blocks of the system model are discussed below.

1. **Input and Preprocessing:** The input to this work is satellite images. The images are taken from United States Geological Survey [102] (as mentioned in Chapter 1) which are high-resolution aerial images. The geometric resolutions of the images are 0.25m, 0.3m, and 0.4m. The capability of the satellite sensor to capture a portion of the surface of the earth is called geometric resolution and is expressed as ground sample distance. Multiple sets of 100 multi-colored images of varying sizes are taken for the work during training. Similarly, for testing, another group of multiple sets of 100 images is taken. For training, the classifiers sets of 100 images of each class for multiple configurations are taken and average results are reported. The image contains three

regions namely sea, house, and grass which are to be segmented. As a preprocessing step, the image is resized to 100×100. The fixed size of the image help in lowering the computational cycles during the prototyping phase as the extensive volume of satellite data is used during training and validation. Then the pixel values are normalized to [0, 1] values. This step is necessary to confine image value distribution to two limits to establish a benchmark configuration. Later on, the values are confined to grayscale which helps the MLP to learn the features better. Further, varying size images are also used for training and testing.

2. **Target:** The target to the system is pixel values of the different regions. If the sea region of the image is to be segmented, then in the image the sea region is selected by keeping pixel values of the region as it is, other values are set to 0. Similarly for the other region also target will be the pixel values of the particular region. This is done using the manual approach. Subsequently, KMC is used to fix the target region.

3. **ANN:** The ANN used, as discussed above, is an MLP trained with BP algorithm. The layers of the MLP have neurons with log- sigmoid and tan-sigmoid activation functions. The MLP configurations have been evaluated with log- sigmoid activation at input and output layers and with tan sigmoid functions in the middle layers.

   As the size of the images is resized to 100×100 and for each region, 100 such RGB images are used, therefore the size of the input matrix to the network is taken as 100×30000. (100 images of size $100 \times 100 \times 3$). Again, the target to the network is the pixel values of the different regions. If the sea region of the image is to be segmented, then in the image the sea region is selected by keeping pixel values of the region as it is, other values are set to 0. Thus for the 100 images size of the target matrix is also 100×30000 (100 target images of size $100 \times 100 \times 3$)

4. **Output:** The output will be pixel values of the region that is to be segmented.

3.2.2   Results and discussion

The work is carried out in a system with CPU @3.3 GHz with RAM of 8 GB with clock frequency 2400 MHz running on Windows 10 platform.

The image used for the experiment and the resized image are shown in Fig. 3.2. The images for the RoIs which are to be segmented are shown in Fig. 3.3. At first, the ANN is trained with five different training functions. The time required for training and MSE between the output and desired images for each training function and each region is calculated. The experimental results are shown in Tables 3.1-3.3. The classifier network forms of BP namely LMBP, CGBP, SGBP, BRBP, and RBP algorithms. The relevant details of these versions of BP have been mentioned in Chapter 2. It has been seen that the training function LMBP is the fastest learning algorithm. As mentioned already MLPs are trained with single, double, and triple hidden layers with different numbers of hidden neurons. Here the training function used is LMBP as it is the fastest (proven from experiments). Then, again MSE between the output image and desired image and the time required for training are calculated for all three regions of the image. The results are shown in Tables 3.4-3.6 below. It is seen that the double hidden layer case of MLP trained with LMBP gives better results than single and triple hidden layered configuration. This indicates better learning and feature capture by the double-layered MLP (with neuron numbers 20 and 10 (Table 3.4)). It requires 90 seconds to train and an MSE convergence of 0.0019 is generated.

From Table 3.1, it is seen that LMBP, produces the best MSE of 0.0058 in 23.78 seconds, SCG gives MSE of 0.0405 in 163.22 seconds, CGBP gives MSE of 0.0638 in 260.52 seconds, BRBP gives MSE of 0.0406 in 42.54 seconds and RBP gives MSE of 0.0924 in 560.61 seconds.

Table 3.1 Experimental results when trained with different training functions for the 'Grass' region

Methods	No. of	Time	MSE

	Hidden Neurons	required in seconds	
Levenberg- Marquardt Back-propagation	10	22.69	0.0438
	20	23.78	0.0058
	30	26.97	0.0065
	40	33.79	0.0072
	50	35.69	0.0079
	60	37.64	0.0147
	70	41.73	0.0230
	80	47.41	0.0310
	90	50.42	0.0469
	100	52.67	0.0582
Scaled conjugate Gradient	10	100.69	0.0616
	20	163.22	0.0405
	30	183.32	0.0525
	40	201.26	0.0613
	50	246.52	0.0724
	60	283.23	0.0795
	70	315.82	0.0823
	80	343.52	0.0914
	90	393.29	0.1058

	100	412.76	0.1267
Conjugate Gradient back-propagation with polak-ribiere updates	10	161.07	0.0734
	20	260.52	0.0638
	30	310.76	0.0679
	40	394.43	0.0731
	50	452.68	0.0774
	60	458.45	0.0795
	70	464.51	0.0847
	80	474.74	0.0891
	90	487.35	0.0925
	100	501.43	0.0962
Bayesian Regulation back-propagation	10	38.62	0.0501
	20	42.54	0.0406
	30	47.12	0.0452
	40	51.47	0.0497
	50	55.62	0.0562
	60	58.92	0.0675
	70	61.16	0.0697
	80	63.65	0.0746
	90	67.52	0.0823
	100	68.12	0.0992

Resilient back-propagation	10	560.61	0.0924
	20	565.48	0.0963
	30	579.12	0.0975
	40	586.58	0.0993
	50	601.82	0.1047
	60	605.13	0.1052
	70	608.42	0.1075
	80	611.25	0.1096
	90	614.31	0.1135
	100	616.52	0.1152

From Table 3.2, it is seen that LMBP, produces the best MSE of 0.0308 in 34.11 seconds, SCG gives MSE of 0.0392 in 428.49 seconds, CGBP gives MSE of 0.0962 in 415.72 seconds, BRBP gives MSE of 0.0562 in 139.62 seconds and RBP gives MSE of 0.0946 in 466.92 seconds.

Table 3.2 Experimental results when trained with different training functions for the 'House' region

Methods	No. of Hidden Neurons	Time required in seconds	MSE
Levenberg- Marquardt Back-propagation	10	29.76	0.0511

	20	34.11	0.0308
	30	39.61	0.0415
	40	44.82	0.0532
	50	51.80	0.0683
	60	52.45	0.0697
	70	53.64	0.0714
	80	55.13	0.0734
	90	56.53	0.0742
	100	57.51	0.0752
	10	446.69	0.0572
Scaled conjugate Gradient	20	428.49	0.0392
	30	431.24	0.0413
	40	443.19	0.0436
	50	450.76	0.0442
	60	453.16	0.0496
	70	455.63	0.0569
	80	456.73	0.0586
	90	459.13	0.0612
	100	461.86	0.0662
	10	405.27	0.1294
Conjugate Gradient back-propagation with polak-ribiere updates	20	415.72	0.0962

	30	421.12	0.1354
	40	428.64	0.1367
	50	432.86	0.1378
	60	434.86	0.1386
	70	436.12	0.1391
	80	436.33	0.1398
	90	437.46	0.1402
	100	440.16	0.1409
	10	133.27	0.0693
Bayesian Regulation back-propagation	20	139.62	0.0562
	30	142.69	0.0578
	40	145.12	0.0586
	50	146.72	0.0598
	60	157.13	0.0618
	70	164.79	0.0624
	80	171.85	0.0654
	90	176.84	0.0667
	100	182.46	0.0687
	10	463.73	0.0952
Resilient back-propagation	20	466.92	0.0946
	30	468.12	0.0957

40	471.32	0.0963
50	474.16	0.0966
60	479.76	0.0972
70	481.16	0.0979
80	483.24	0.0985
90	485.46	0.0993
100	488.72	0.1012

From Table 3.3, it is seen that LMBP, produces the best MSE of 0.0160 in 30.25 seconds, SCG gives MSE of 0.0956 in 346.80 seconds, CGBP gives MSE of 0.09860 in 326.72 seconds, BRBP gives MSE of 0.0642 in 102.76 seconds and RBP gives MSE of 470.16 in 0.0942 seconds.

Table 3.3 Experimental results when trained with different training functions for 'Sea' region

Methods	No. of Hidden Neurons	Time required in seconds	MSE
	10	44.65	0.0868
Levenberg- Marquardt Back-propagation	20	30.25	0.0160
	30	35.76	0.0231
	40	37.56	0.0342
	50	41.71	0.0362

	60	44.69	0.0392
	70	47.79	0.0467
	80	51.76	0.0586
	90	56.35	0.0634
	100	64.33	0.0765
Scaled conjugate Gradient	10	335.79	0.0969
	20	346.80	0.0956
	30	357.24	0.0964
	40	364.58	0.0978
	50	371.56	0.0989
	60	376.89	0.0997
	70	383.52	0.1069
	80	385.63	0.1087
	90	389.75	0.1113
	100	392.10	0.1146
Conjugate Gradient back-propagation with polak-ribiere updates	10	315.46	0.0995
	20	326.72	0.0986
	30	330.12	0.0989
	40	334.67	0.0991
	50	338.69	0.0997
	60	341.19	0.1057

	70	343.56	0.1075
	80	345.65	0.1123
	90	349.19	0.1156
	100	350.18	0.1279
	10	99.96	0.0667
Bayesian Regulation back-propagation	20	102.76	0.0642
	30	105.54	0.0668
	40	113.75	0.0679
	50	118.24	0.0689
	60	148.65	0.0697
	70	179.57	0.0712
	80	218.86	0.0739
	90	268.77	0.0740
	100	315.45	0.0646
	10	462.86	0.0946
Resilient back-propagation	20	470.16	0.0942
	30	472.46	0.0946
	40	475.36	0.0952
	50	476.21	0.0956
	60	476.451	0.0965
	70	477.11	0.0976

80	478.54	0.0987
90	480.31	0.0996
100	482.13	0.1030

The results of MLP training for the work obtained using LMBP, SCG, CGBP, BRBP and RBP training functions with a single hidden layer for all the regions, (Grass, House, Sea) given in Tables 3.1 to 3.3 indicates that LMBP is the best training approach. The number of hidden neurons at first is taken as 10 and increased gradually with the step of 10. In most of the cases, it was seen that when the hidden neuron number is taken as 20 it gives better results in terms of MSE. When the hidden neuron is increased further the MSE value also increases. Therefore for all the training functions, the hidden neuron number is taken from 10 to 100 in the steps of 10.

From the Tables 3.1 to 3.3, it is seen that the LMBP algorithm required less time (around 20 seconds when the number of the hidden neuron is 10 and 60 seconds when hidden neuron number is 100). MSE for the LMBP algorithm is different for different regions. For the 'Grass' region, MSE is around 0.0058 to 0.0582 depending upon the number of hidden neurons. Similarly, for the 'House' region MSE is around 0.0308 to 0.0752 and for the 'Sea' region MSE is around 0.0160 to 0.0868. For the other training functions, the MSE value calculated is much higher than LMBP. For SCG, the MSE value is around 0.0392 to 0.1267 depending upon the number of hidden neurons and the type of region selected for training. Similarly for the CGBP algorithm, the MSE calculated is around 0.0638 to 0.1409, for BRBP, around 0.0406 to 0.0992 and for RBP training, it was around 0.0924 to 0.1152. The time required for computation for these functions was also much higher than LMBP (around 40 to 600 seconds).

(a) Input Image

(b) Resized Image

Fig. 3.2 Example of Input and Resized image

(a) Grass region   (b) House region   (c) Sea region

Fig. 3.3 RoIs for Grass, House and Sea region

(a) Grass region   (b) House region   (c) Sea region

Fig. 3.4 Output images for Grass, House and Sea region

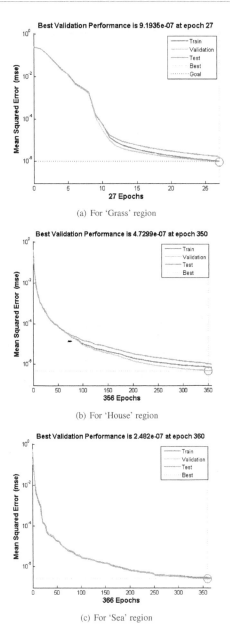

(a) For 'Grass' region

(b) For 'House' region

(c) For 'Sea' region

Fig. 3.5 MSE convergence graph when trained with MLP with the double hidden layer for 'Grass', 'House' and 'Sea' regions

Subsequently, as LMBP has been established to be fastest, it is used to train single, double, and triple hidden layer MLP for 'Grass', 'House' and 'Sea' regions are shown in Tables 3.4 to 3.6. The MSE convergence curve when trained with MLP with double hidden layers for all the three regions are shown in Fig. 3.5

From Table 3.4, it is seen that the best MSE for the single hidden layer is 0.0058 in 23.78 seconds, for the double hidden layer is 0.0019 in 90.34 seconds and for three hidden layers is 0.0341 in 197.19 seconds.

Table 3.4 Experimental results when trained with single, double, and triple hidden layer for 'Grass' region (trained with LMBP).

ANN with different size of hidden layer	No. of Hidden Neurons	Time required in seconds	MSE
	10	22.69	0.0438
ANN with single hidden layer	20	23.78	0.0058
	30	26.97	0.0065
	40	33.79	0.0072
	50	35.69	0.0079
	60	37.64	0.0147
	70	41.73	0.0230
	80	47.41	0.0310
	90	50.42	0.0469
	100	52.67	0.0582
ANN with double hidden layer	[10 10]	57.94	0.0134

[10 20]	61.19	0.0132
[10 30]	64.24	0.0156
[10 40]	69.54	0.0145
[10 50]	72.45	0.0146
[10 60]	74.14	0.0167
[10 70]	78.35	0.0175
[10 80]	81.34	0.0178
[10 90]	85.26	0.0186
[10 100]	88.14	0.0190
[20 10]	90.34	0.0019
[20 20]	93.14	0.0020
[20 30]	96.36	0.0023
[20 40]	97.12	0.0026
[20 50]	109.83	0.0027
[20 60]	113.94	0.0035
[20 70]	114.16	0.0041
[20 80]	117.56	0.0047
[20 90]	118.46	0.0058
[20 100]	121.35	0.0079
[30 10]	124.94	0.0089
[30 20]	131.76	0.0092

	[30 30]	134.35	0.0105
	[30 40]	142.43	0.00114
	[30 50]	150.23	0.0121
ANN with triple hidden layer	[10 10 10]	197.19	0.0341
	[10 10 20]	213.45	0.0346
	[10 10 30]	214.64	0.0367
	[10 10 40]	216.75	0.0374
	[10 10 50]	258.67	0.0378
	[10 20 10]	268.35	0.0413
	[10 20 20]	271.45	0.0425
	[10 20 30]	273.65	0.0435
	[10 20 40]	275.64	0.0446
	[10 20 50]	287.12	0.0465
	[10 30 10]	284.21	0.0478
	[10 30 20]	290.23	0.0486
	[10 30 30]	293.34	0.0495
	[10 30 40]	296.45	0.0513
	[10 30 50]	312.67	0.0523
	[20 10 10]	321.47	0.0536
	[20 10 20]	323.24	0.0546
	[20 10 30]	325.25	0.0579

[20 10 40]	328.15	0.0582
[20 10 50]	329.17	0.0589
[20 20 10]	333.15	0.0601
[20 20 20]	345.64	0.0613
[20 20 30]	351.19	0.0623
[20 20 40]	353.54	0.0641

From Table 3.5, when MLP is trained for the 'House' region it is seen that the best MSE for the single hidden layer is 0.03080 in 34.11 seconds, for the double hidden layer is 0.02190 in 92.54 seconds and for three hidden layers is 0.0431 in 187.69 seconds.

Table 3.5 Experimental results when trained with single, double, and triple hidden layer for the 'House' region (trained with LMBP).

ANN with different size of hidden layer	No. of Hidden Neurons	Time required in seconds	MSE
	10	29.76	0.0511
ANN with single hidden layer	20	34.11	0.0308
	30	39.61	0.0415
	40	44.82	0.0532
	50	51.80	0.0683
	60	52.45	0.0697

70	53.64	0.0714
80	55.13	0.0734
90	56.53	0.0742
100	57.51	0.0752
ANN with double hidden layer	[10 10]	55.92	0.0431
[10 20]	60.39	0.0442
[10 30]	63.29	0.0456
[10 40]	66.24	0.0467
[10 50]	70.44	0.0478
[10 60]	73.11	0.0482
[10 70]	76.34	0.0483
[10 80]	82.14	0.0487
[10 90]	86.23	0.0489
[10 100]	89.44	0.0490
[20 10]	92.54	0.0219
[20 20]	94.16	0.0223
[20 30]	97.36	0.0225
[20 40]	99.72	0.0227
[20 50]	108.43	0.0029
[20 60]	112.14	0.0235
[20 70]	113.76	0.0241

	[20 80]	115.46	0.0247
	[20 90]	117.76	0.0258
	[20 100]	120.55	0.0279
	[30 10]	123.24	0.0389
	[30 20]	130.66	0.0392
	[30 30]	133.65	0.0405
	[30 40]	140.83	0.00414
	[30 50]	146.73	0.0421
ANN with triple hidden layer	[10 10 10]	187.69	0.0431
	[10 10 20]	203.55	0.0436
	[10 10 30]	214.74	0.0457
	[10 10 40]	226.55	0.0464
	[10 10 50]	248.47	0.0468
	[10 20 10]	258.25	0.0503
	[10 20 20]	261.25	0.0515
	[10 20 30]	263.45	0.0525
	[10 20 40]	265.84	0.0536
	[10 20 50]	277.92	0.0545
	[10 30 10]	274.31	0.0558
	[10 30 20]	280.73	0.0566
	[10 30 30]	293.44	0.0575

[10 30 40]	296.15	0.0603
[10 30 50]	302.47	0.0613
[20 10 10]	311.27	0.0626
[20 10 20]	313.34	0.0636
[20 10 30]	315.35	0.0649
[20 10 40]	318.15	0.0652
[20 10 50]	319.67	0.0669
[20 20 10]	323.25	0.0711
[20 20 20]	335.44	0.0723
[20 20 30]	341.69	0.0733
[20 20 40]	343.74	0.0741

From Table 3.6, when MLP is trained for the 'Sea' region it is seen that the best MSE for the single hidden layer is 0.0160 in 30.25 seconds, for the double hidden layer is 0.01140 in 82.44 seconds and for three hidden layers is 0.0533 in 137.39 seconds.

Table 3.6 Experimental results when trained with single, double, and triple hidden layer for 'Sea' region (trained with LMBP)

ANN with different size of hidden layer	No. of Hidden Neurons	Time required in seconds	MSE
	10	44.65	0.0868
ANN with single hidden layer			

	20	30.25	0.0160
	30	35.76	0.0231
	40	37.56	0.0342
	50	41.71	0.0362
	60	44.69	0.0392
	70	47.79	0.0467
	80	51.76	0.0586
	90	56.35	0.0634
	100	64.33	0.0765
ANN with double hidden layer	[10 10]	57.12	0.0214
	[10 20]	60.79	0.0246
	[10 30]	62.19	0.0252
	[10 40]	63.64	0.0268
	[10 50]	67.54	0.0272
	[10 60]	70.41	0.0283
	[10 70]	72.44	0.0287
	[10 80]	75.54	0.0288
	[10 90]	76.83	0.0289
	[10 100]	79.64	0.0293
	[20 10]	82.44	0.0114
	[20 20]	84.66	0.0123

	[20 30]	87.46	0.0125
	[20 40]	89.62	0.0127
	[20 50]	98.63	0.0129
	[20 60]	102.74	0.0135
	[20 70]	103.77	0.0141
	[20 80]	105.36	0.0147
	[20 90]	107.66	0.0158
	[20 100]	129.65	0.0179
	[30 10]	133.54	0.0359
	[30 20]	140.56	0.0362
	[30 30]	143.85	0.0375
	[30 40]	150.73	0.00384
	[30 50]	156.73	0.0391
ANN with triple hidden layer	[10 10 10]	137.39	0.0533
	[10 10 20]	213.45	0.0537
	[10 10 30]	224.64	0.0546
	[10 10 40]	236.45	0.0563
	[10 10 50]	238.37	0.0575
	[10 20 10]	248.25	0.0601
	[10 20 20]	251.55	0.0613
	[10 20 30]	253.75	0.0624

[10 20 40]	255.34	0.0633
[10 20 50]	267.42	0.0642
[10 30 10]	274.81	0.0653
[10 30 20]	277.53	0.0664
[10 30 30]	283.84	0.0672
[10 30 40]	286.45	0.0701
[10 30 50]	292.77	0.0712
[20 10 10]	301.37	0.0724
[20 10 20]	314.14	0.0733
[20 10 30]	316.75	0.0744
[20 10 40]	318.35	0.0753
[20 10 50]	321.67	0.0765
[20 20 10]	323.45	0.0814
[20 20 20]	326.34	0.0825
[20 20 30]	335.29	0.0832
[20 20 40]	343.34	0.0844

As the LMBP algorithm gives better results in terms of MSE and computational time than the other training functions, the ANN is now trained with double and triple hidden layers with LMBP as the training algorithm (Table 3.4-3.6). For a single hidden layer at first, the number of the hidden neuron is kept as 10 in the first hidden layer and for the second hidden

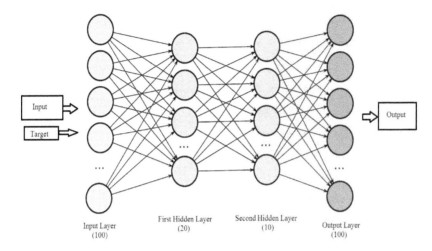

Fig. 3.6 Architecture of the MLP with double hidden layer

layer, it is increased gradually with steps of 10. As the MSE value also increases gradually with these set of values, therefore the hidden neuron number is increased to 20 in the first hidden layer and again it is increased gradually in the second layer with steps of 10. In this way, the number of hidden neurons is altered and the MSE value is calculated for each case. In the case of the double hidden layer, at first, the number of hidden neurons is kept as 10 in the first layer, and in the second layer, it is increased gradually with steps of 10. As the MSE value also increases gradually with these set of values, therefore the hidden neuron number is increased to 20 in the first layer and again it is increased gradually in the second layer with steps of 10. In this way, the number of hidden neuron numbers is altered and the MSE value is calculated for each case. Similarly for the three hidden layers combination also, at first the numbers of hidden neurons in the first and second layer are kept at 10, and in the third layer, it is increased gradually with steps of 10. Then keeping the first hidden layer neuron number as it is, the second hidden layer neuron number is increased to 20 and the third hidden layer neuron numbers are increased gradually with steps of 10. In this way, by changing the number of hidden neuron numbers the MSE value is calculated for three hidden layer combinations also. From the experimental results, it is seen that the double hidden layer gives better results than the triple-layer and single layer. This procedure for selecting hidden neuron layer and neuron number also helps to avoid overfitting. The minimum value of MSE value for double layer MLP for the 'Grass' region is calculated to be 0.0019, for the 'House' region it is 0.0219 and for the 'Sea' region it is 0.0114. For the triple hidden layer, the MSE values vary from 0.0341 to 0.0844 depending on the number of hidden neurons in the hidden layers and RoI selected for training. There is an improvement of 9.52 times in the minimum MSE value with two hidden layers and 1.8 times betterment of minimum MSE value in case of three-layer MLP between lower and higher MSE (recorded average) limits for 'Grass', 'House and 'Sea' regions. This is verified in validation steps. Depending upon this result, the two hidden layer MLP trained with LMBP is taken to be the most suitable network. The best performance given by MLPs of different configurations for 'Grass', 'house' and 'sea' regions with manual RoI selection is shown in Table 3.7. The architecture of MLP with a double hidden layer is shown in Fig. 3.6.

Table 3.7 The best performance given by MLPs of different configurations for 'Grass', 'house', and 'sea' regions with manual RoI selection.

MLP configuration	'Grass' Region		'House' Region		'Sea' region	
	MSE	Time required in Seconds	MSE	Time required in Seconds	MSE	Time required in Seconds
Single hidden layer	0.058	23.78	0.03080	34.11	0.0160	30.25
Double hidden layer	0.0019	90.34	0.0219	92.54	0.0114	82.44
Triple hidden layer	0.0341	197.19	.0431	187.69	0.0533	137.39

3.3   Satellite Image Segmentation based on ANN and KMC

The method discussed in Section 3.2 requires manual intervention to select the RoI which has been used as the target to train the MLP. This is not preferable in all situations. However, to automate the approach, there should not be any human intervention. To make the approach automated during training irrespective of texture, size, distribution, and color of the image, a KMC based RoI identification method is proposed here. The identified RoI is used for MLP training. This method of segmentation of satellite images in complex backgrounds is found to be effective. The work considers the formation and training of an ANN in which the output of the KMC algorithm is used to label the particular RoIs in the image, and the region is used as the target. The method does not require any feature extraction, region growing or splitting methods to configure and train an ANN, which for the work is an MLP trained with (error) BP based learning [2].

3.3.1   System model

The block diagram for the proposed method is shown in Fig. 3.7 The block diagram and the steps involved in the method are explained below.

1. The input in this work is satellite images. The images are taken from United States Geological Survey [102], which are high-resolution aerial images. The description included in step 1 of Section 3.2.1 is also relevant here. The image contains three regions namely 'Sea', 'House' and 'Grass' which are to be segmented.

2. The image is then converted to $L \times a \times b$ color space. The $L \times a \times b$ color space was derived from the international commission on illumination (CIE) XYZ tristimulus

---

[2]A part of this work is reported in

1. M. Barthakur and K.K. Sarma, Complex Image Segmentation using K-means Clustering Aided Neuro-computing, in proceedings of Fifth IEEE International Conference on Signal Processing and integrated networks (SPIN), Noida, New Delhi, Feb.,2018.

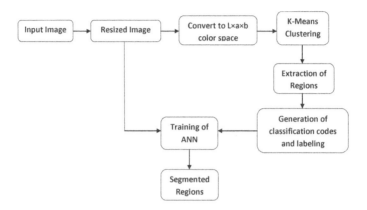

Fig. 3.7 System model of the method

values. The $L \times a \times b$ space consists of a luminosity layer 'L', chromaticity-layer 'a' indicating where the color falls along the red-green axis, and chromaticity-layer 'b' indicating where the color falls along the blue-yellow axis. Since all of the color information is in the 'a' and 'b' layers, the 'a' and 'b' values of the pixels are taken for further processing.

3. Then the KMC algorithm is applied to cluster different regions of the image. Here, the grouping is done by minimizing the Euclidean distances between data and the corresponding cluster center.

4. The algorithm returns an index corresponding to a cluster in the image and with these index values, every pixel in the image is labeled.

5. Using the labeled pixels, the RoI of the image is separated.

6. Using the RoI as target and the resized image of Step 1 as input, the MLPs are trained with BP algorithm as explained in Section 3.2. The batch training method is adopted as it accelerates the speed of training and the rate of convergence of the MSE to the desired value. At first, the MLP is trained with one hidden layer with different training functions and then it is trained with two and three hidden layers. The input and output layers use log-sigmoid activation while the hidden layers use tan-sigmoid activation functions.

7. The output of the ANN will be pixel values of the region that is to be segmented.

3.3.2   Results and discussion

The method is tested using satellite images. The images are shown in Fig. 3.8. The image is used to segment the ''Grass', 'House', and 'Sea' region of the image (Fig. 3.9). At first, the ANN is trained with different training functions. Then MSE between the output image and desired image for each training function has been calculated. The experimental results are shown in Tables 3.8, 3.10 and 3.12. The classifier network is trained with five different forms of BP namely LMBP, CGBP, SGBP, BRBP, and RBP. It has been seen that the training function LMBP gives better results than other functions. Then the MLP is trained with single, double, and triple hidden layers with different numbers of hidden neurons. Here the training function used is LMBP as it is the fastest. Then, again MSE between the output image and the desired image is calculated for both the images. The results are shown in Tables 3.9, 3.11 and 3.13 below. It is seen that the double hidden layer case gives better results. The outputs of the ANN are shown in Fig. 3.10 and the MSE convergence graph for all the regions, when trained with MLP with double hidden layer, are shown in Fig. 3.11.

From Table 3.8, it is seen that for the 'Grass' region when trained with LMBP, the MLP produces the best MSE of 0.0055 in 21.39 seconds, SCG gives MSE of 0.0478 in 114.15

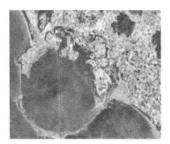

Fig. 3.8 Example of Input image

(a) 'Grass' region   (b) 'House' region   (c) 'Sea' region

Fig. 3.9 RoIs for 'Grass', 'House' and 'Sea' regions

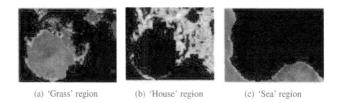

(a) 'Grass' region   (b) 'House' region   (c) 'Sea' region

Fig. 3.10 Output images for 'Grass', 'House' and 'Sea' region

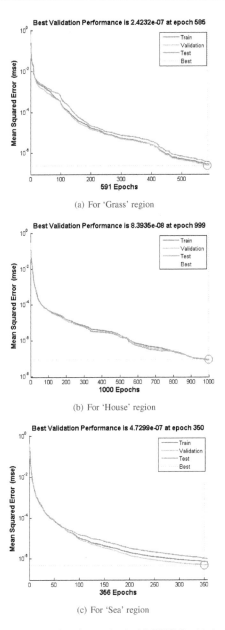

(a) For 'Grass' region

(b) For 'House' region

(c) For 'Sea' region

Fig. 3.11 MSE convergence graphs when trained with FFMLP with double hidden layer for 'Grass', 'House' and 'Sea' regions

seconds, CGBP gives MSE of 0.0624 in 207.62 seconds, BRBP gives MSE of 0.0416 in 102.76 seconds and RBP gives MSE of 0.0914 in 513.31 seconds.

Table 3.8 Experimental results when trained with different training functions for the 'Grass' region

Methods	No. of Hidden Neurons	Time required in seconds	MSE
Levenberg- Marquardt Back-propagation	10	20.72	0.0331
	20	21.39	0.0055
	30	23.55	0.0062
	40	31.89	0.0065
	50	33.99	0.0074
	60	35.68	0.0127
	70	40.43	0.0210
	80	45.71	0.0306
	90	50.12	0.0449
	100	52.57	0.0482
Scaled conjugate Gradient	10	90.65	0.0516
	20	114.15	0.0478
	30	135.62	0.0505
	40	155.26	0.0587
	50	178.52	0.0656

	60	180.23	0.0713
	70	205.82	0.0796
	80	223.52	0.0844
	90	253.29	0.965
	100	302.76	0.0987
	10	151.17	0.0714
Conjugate Gradient back-propagation with polak-ribiere updates	20	207.62	0.0624
	30	252.56	0.0667
	40	294.53	0.0725
	50	352.78	0.0765
	60	408.15	0.0787
	70	444.71	0.0812
	80	464.75	0.0878
	90	483.25	0.0923
	100	511.23	0.0945
	10	36.12	0.0495
Bayesian Regulation back-propagation	20	40.44	0.0416
	30	46.32	0.0458
	40	48.17	0.0464
	50	54.22	0.0556
	60	58.45	0.0645

	70	60.65	0.0685
	80	63.78	0.0734
	90	65.67	0.0835
	100	69.34	0.0972
	10	513.31	0.0914
Resilient back-propagation	20	545.43	0.0933
	30	534.62	0.0955
	40	545.48	0.0986
	50	595.82	0.0995
	60	615.15	0.1032
	70	618.32	0.1055
	80	621.67	0.1076
	90	624.51	0.1124
	100	626.86	0.1132

From Table 3.9, when MLP is trained for the 'Grass' region it is seen that the best MSE for the single hidden layer is 0.0055 in 21.39 seconds, for the double hidden layer is 0.0018 in 88.24 seconds and for three hidden layers is 0.0339 in 193.29 seconds.

Table 3.9 Experimental results when trained with single, double, and triple hidden layer for the 'Grass' region.

ANN with different size	No. of Hidden	Time required	MSE

of hidden layers	Neurons	in	
		seconds	
	10	20.72	0.0331
ANN with single hidden layer	20	21.39	0.0055
	30	23.55	0.0062
	40	31.89	0.0065
	50	33.99	0.0074
	60	35.68	0.0127
	70	40.43	0.0210
	80	45.71	0.0306
	90	50.12	0.0449
	100	52.57	0.0482
ANN with double hidden layer	[10 10]	55.84	0.0132
	[10 20]	60.29	0.0130
	[10 30]	63.14	0.0154
	[10 40]	67.53	0.0141
	[10 50]	70.42	0.0143
	[10 60]	72.10	0.0163
	[10 70]	74.32	0.0173
	[10 80]	78.14	0.0175
	[10 90]	83.21	0.0184

	[10 100]	84.11	0.0189
	[20 10]	88.24	0.0018
	[20 20]	90.11	0.0019
	[20 30]	93.32	0.0022
	[20 40]	95.11	0.0024
	[20 50]	103.13	0.0026
	[20 60]	110.13	0.0033
	[20 70]	112.11	0.0040
	[20 80]	115.53	0.0045
	[20 90]	116.42	0.0055
	[20 100]	120.33	0.0076
	[30 10]	122.24	0.0087
	[30 20]	128.26	0.0090
	[30 30]	132.31	0.097
	[30 40]	139.71	0.0111
ANN with triple hidden layer	[10 10 10]	193.29	0.0339
	[10 10 20]	203.44	0.0342
	[10 10 30]	212.34	0.0357
	[10 10 40]	213.74	0.0364
	[10 10 50]	253.66	0.0368
	[10 20 10]	266.33	0.0386

[10 20 20]	269.15	0.0415
[10 20 30]	272.63	0.0426
[10 20 40]	274.62	0.0437
[10 20 50]	286.22	0.0448
[10 30 10]	287.31	0.0459
[10 30 20]	293.13	0.0476
[10 30 30]	294.24	0.0485
[10 30 40]	294.45	0.0503
[10 30 50]	302.37	0.0513
[20 10 10]	311.37	0.0526
[20 10 20]	320.25	0.0536
[20 10 30]	323.23	0.0549
[20 10 40]	325.12	0.0562
[20 10 50]	327.14	0.0579
[20 20 10]	330.16	0.0611
[20 20 20]	336.44	0.0613
[20 20 30]	345.12	0.0619
[20 20 40]	352.54	0.0631

From Table 3.10, it is seen that for the 'House' region when trained with LMBP, the MLP with LMBP, produces the best MSE of 0.0318 in 33.51 seconds, SCG gives MSE of 0.0382 in 418.35 seconds, CGBP gives MSE of 0.0952 in 410.42 seconds, BRBP gives MSE of 0.0552 in 136.12 seconds and RBP gives MSE of 0.0926 in 454.92 seconds.

Table 3.10 Experimental results when trained with different training functions for the 'House' region

Methods	No. of Hidden Neurons	Time required in seconds	MSE
Levenberg- Marquardt Back-propagation	10	29.16	0.0411
	20	33.51	0.0318
	30	35.21	0.0405
	40	43.83	0.0432
	50	50.60	0.0553
	60	51.43	0.0597
	70	55.14	0.0664
	80	56.12	0.0714
	90	56.78	0.0732
	100	57.11	0.0745
Scaled conjugate Gradient	10	403.65	0.0472
	20	418.35	0.0382
	30	421.25	0.0403
	40	433.59	0.0426
	50	446.16	0.0432

	60	450.46	0.0476
	70	452.33	0.0549
	80	455.45	0.0556
	90	458.46	0.0602
	100	460.46	0.0642
Conjugate Gradient back-propagation with polak-ribiere updates	10	397.23	0.1134
	20	410.42	0.0952
	30	425.15	0.1244
	40	426.24	0.1267
	50	431.46	0.1308
	60	434.26	0.1346
	70	435.13	0.1351
	80	435.73	0.1378
	90	436.56	0.1392
	100	438.16	0.1405
Bayesian Regulation back-propagation	10	130.27	0.0593
	20	136.12	0.0552
	30	140.49	0.0568
	40	142.52	0.0576
	50	143.62	0.0588
	60	155.23	0.0608

	70	160.49	0.0614
	80	165.15	0.0625
	90	170.34	0.0635
	100	178.46	0.0648
	10	435.73	0.0942
Resilient back-propagation	20	454.92	0.0926
	30	457.72	0.0967
	40	465.42	0.0973
	50	473.56	0.0976
	60	475.66	0.0982
	70	480.56	0.0989
	80	482.14	0.0992
	90	484.36	0.0993
	100	488.12	0.1002

From Table 3.11, when MLP is trained for the 'House' region it is seen that the best MSE for the single hidden layer is 0.0318 in 33.51 seconds, for the double hidden layer is 0.0215 in 90.14 seconds and for three hidden layers is 0.0446 in 180.62 seconds.

Table 3.11 Experimental results when trained with single, double, and triple hidden layer for the 'House' region.

ANN with different size	No. of Hidden	Time required	MSE

of hidden layer	Neurons	in seconds	
		seconds	
ANN with single hidden layer	10	29.16	0.0411
	20	33.51	0.0318
	30	35.21	0.0405
	40	43.83	0.0432
	50	50.60	0.0553
	60	51.43	0.0597
	70	55.14	0.0664
	80	56.12	0.0714
	90	56.78	0.0732
	100	57.11	0.0745
ANN with double hidden layer	[10 10]	54.12	0.0426
	[10 20]	58.29	0.0435
	[10 30]	60.49	0.0446
	[10 40]	63.14	0.0456
	[10 50]	69.14	0.0469
	[10 60]	70.35	0.0475
	[10 70]	74.46	0.0480
	[10 80]	80.74	0.0486
	[10 90]	85.73	0.0484

	[10 100]	88.44	0.0487
	[20 10]	90.14	0.0215
	[20 20]	93.46	0.0219
	[20 30]	95.26	0.0223
	[20 40]	97.42	0.0225
	[20 50]	103.53	0.0226
	[20 60]	109.64	0.0233
	[20 70]	112.56	0.0240
	[20 80]	113.16	0.0245
	[20 90]	114.66	0.0256
	[20 100]	116.45	0.0268
	[30 10]	127.74	0.0375
	[30 20]	130.16	0.0387
	[30 30]	132.55	0.0400
	[30 40]	138.53	0.00409
	[30 50]	147.33	0.0418
ANN with triple hidden layer	[10 10 10]	180.62	0.0446
	[10 10 20]	197.53	0.0457
	[10 10 30]	208.64	0.0468
	[10 10 40]	216.56	0.0475
	[10 10 50]	238.67	0.0483

[10 20 10]	267.45	0.0495
[10 20 20]	269.23	0.0505
[10 20 30]	275.43	0.0513
[10 20 40]	276.24	0.0524
[10 20 50]	277.12	0.0538
[10 30 10]	273.21	0.0542
[10 30 20]	279.13	0.0549
[10 30 30]	283.56	0.0555
[10 30 40]	290.45	0.0596
[10 30 50]	298.37	0.0603
[20 10 10]	308.17	0.0616
[20 10 20]	312.14	0.0626
[20 10 30]	314.65	0.0627
[20 10 40]	315.35	0.0636
[20 10 50]	316.37	0.0648
[20 20 10]	320.15	0.0706
[20 20 20]	328.24	0.0713
[20 20 30]	336.64	0.0726
[20 20 40]	340.64	0.0735

From Table 3.12, it is seen that when trained for the 'Sea' region with LMBP, the MLP produces the best MSE of 0.0145 in 27.35 seconds, SCG gives MSE of 0.0945 in 326.72 seconds, CGBP gives MSE of 0.0946 in 316.72 seconds, BRBP gives MSE of 0.0632 in 100.76 seconds and RBP gives MSE of 0.0926 in 432.36 seconds.

Table 3.12 Experimental results when trained with different training functions for the 'Sea' region

Methods	No. of Hidden Neurons	Time required in seconds	MSE
Levenberg- Marquardt Back-propagation	10	43.15	0.0568
	20	27.35	0.0145
	30	33.46	0.0221
	40	35.76	0.0332
	50	40.31	0.0342
	60	43.49	0.0387
	70	45.69	0.0457
	80	50.36	0.0575
	90	56.15	0.0624
	100	65.313	0.0746
Scaled conjugate Gradient	10	315.19	0.0915
	20	326.40	0.0947
	30	367.34	0.0936

	40	324.48	0.0957
	50	351.16	0.0978
	60	346.59	0.098597
	70	313.32	0.1009
	80	325.43	0.1067
	90	349.55	0.1102
	100	352.10	0.1135
Conjugate Gradient back-propagation with polak-ribiere updates	10	315.46	0.0967
	20	316.72	0.0946
	30	330.12	0.0978
	40	334.67	0.0988
	50	338.69	0.0990
	60	341.19	0.1047
	70	343.56	0.1065
	80	345.65	0.1124
	90	349.19	0.11466
	100	350.18	0.1264
Bayesian Regulation back-propagation	10	94.96	0.0664
	20	100.76	0.0632
	30	103.54	0.0648
	40	107.75	0.0675

	50	115.24	0.0680
	60	138.55	0.0695
	70	151.77	0.0710
	80	212.87	0.0734
	90	264.67	0.0733
	100	314.25	0.0716
	10	432.36	0.0926
Resilient back-propagation	20	440.36	0.0945
	30	468.46	0.0947
	40	474.36	0.0950
	50	477.21	0.0954
	60	478.61	0.0960
	70	478.11	0.0975
	80	478.24	0.0984
	90	479.41	0.0994
	100	481.63	0.1013

From Table 3.13, when MLP is trained for the 'Sea' region it is seen that the best MSE for the single hidden layer is 0.0145 in 27.35 seconds, for the double hidden layer is 0.0104 in 81.35 seconds and for three hidden layers is 0.0546 in 137.39 seconds.

Table 3.13 Experimental results when trained with single, double, and triple hidden layer for the 'Sea' region.

ANN with different size of hidden layer	No. of Hidden Neurons	Time required in seconds	MSE
	10	43.15	0.0568
ANN with single hidden layer	20	27.35	0.0145
	30	33.46	0.0221
	40	35.76	0.0332
	50	40.31	0.0342
	60	43.49	0.0387
	70	45.69	0.0457
	80	50.36	0.0575
	90	56.15	0.0624
	100	65.313	0.0746
ANN with double hidden layer	[10 10]	55.10	0.0245
	[10 20]	59.12	0.0267
	[10 30]	60.49	0.0278
	[10 40]	62.44	0.0288
	[10 50]	66.34	0.0297
	[10 60]	69.45	0.0302
	[10 70]	71.34	0.0312

	[10 80]	74.34	0.0324
	[10 90]	75.13	0.0331
	[10 100]	76.46	0.0342
	[20 10]	81.35	0.0104
	[20 20]	83.26	0.0113
	[20 30]	85.36	0.0134
	[20 40]	85.22	0.0143
	[20 50]	95.34	0.0146
	[20 60]	100.24	0.0148
	[20 70]	102.17	0.0149
	[20 80]	103.16	0.0152
	[20 90]	105.16	0.0158
	[20 100]	120.35	0.0164
	[30 10]	133.51	0.0335
	[30 20]	138.14	0.0323
	[30 30]	145.64	0.0356
	[30 40]	148.70	0.0374
	[30 50]	153.13	0.0383
ANN with triple hidden layer	[10 10 10]	137.39	0.0546
	[10 10 20]	232.55	0.0548
	[10 10 30]	235.45	0.0550

[10 10 40]	239.24	0.0555
[10 10 50]	240.17	0.0558
[10 20 10]	241.32	0.0623
[10 20 20]	246.15	0.0646
[10 20 30]	257.45	0.0665
[10 20 40]	260.12	0.0683
[10 20 50]	262.13	0.0702
[10 30 10]	274.11	0.0724
[10 30 20]	280.52	0.0746
[10 30 30]	286.23	0.0765
[10 30 40]	288.25	0.0782
[10 30 50]	295.25	0.0795
[20 10 10]	313.47	0.0804
[20 10 20]	317.65	0.0814
[20 10 30]	321.76	0.0834
[20 10 40]	327.25	0.0854
[20 10 50]	335.34	0.0865
[20 20 10]	345.12	0.0887
[20 20 20]	346.45	0.0896
[20 20 30]	351.35	0.0902
[20 20 40]	355.24	0.0914

At first, (from Tables 3.8, 3.10 and 3.12), ANN is trained with LMBP, SCG, CGBP, BRBP and RBP training functions with single hidden layer for all the regions, (Grass, House, Sea). The number of hidden neurons at first is taken as 10 and increased gradually with the step of 10. In most cases, it is seen that when the hidden neuron number is taken as 20 it gives better results in terms of MSE. When the hidden neuron is increased further the MSE value also increases. Therefore for all the training functions, the hidden neuron number is taken from 10 to 100 in the steps of 10.

From the Tables 3.8,3.10 and 3.12 it is seen that LMBP algorithm require less time (around 20 seconds when number of hidden neuron is 10 and 60 seconds when hidden neuron number is 100). MSE for LMBP is different for different regions. For the 'Grass' region, MSE is around 0.0311 to 0.0482 depending upon the number of hidden neurons. Similarly, for the 'House' region MSE is around 0.0411 to 0.0745 and for the 'Sea' region it is around 0.145 to 0.746. For the other training functions, the MSE value calculated is much higher than LMBP. For SCG, the MSE value is around 0.0472 to 0.0987 depending upon the number of hidden neurons and the type of region selected for training. Similarly for CGBP, the MSE calculated is around 0.0624 to 0.1405, for BRBP, around 0.0416 to 0.0972 and for RBP training, it was around 0.0914 to 0.1132. The time required for computation for these functions was also much higher than LMBP (around 20 to 600 seconds).

As LMBP algorithm gives better results in terms of MSE and computational time than the other training functions, therefore the ANN is now trained with double and triple hidden layers with LMBP as training algorithm (Tables 3.9, 3.11 and 3.13). In the case of the double hidden layer, at first, the number of hidden neurons is kept as 10 in the first layer, and in the second layer, it is increased gradually with steps of 10. As the MSE value also increases gradually with these set of values, therefore the hidden neuron number is increased to 20 in the first layer and again it is increased gradually in the second layer with steps of 10. In this way, the number of hidden neuron numbers is altered and the MSE value is calculated for each case. Similarly for three hidden layer combinations also, at first the number of hidden neurons in the first and second layer are kept at 10, and in the third layer, it is increased gradually with steps of 10. Then keeping the first hidden layer neuron number as it is, the second hidden layer neuron number is increased to 20 and the third hidden layer neuron numbers are increased gradually with steps of 10. In this way, by changing the number of hidden neuron numbers the MSE value is calculated for three hidden layer combinations also. From the experimental results, it is seen that the double hidden layer gives better results than the triple-layer and single layer. The minimum value of MSE value for double layer MLP in the 'Grass' region is calculated as around 0.0018, for the 'House' region it is 0.0215 and for'Sea' region it is 0.0104. For the triple hidden layer, the MSE values vary from 0.0339 to 0.0914 depending on the number of hidden neurons in the hidden layers and RoI selected for training. There is an improvement of 10.9 times in the minimum MSE value with two hidden layers and 1.6 times betterment of minimum MSE value in case of three-layer MLP between lower and higher MSE (recorded average) limits for 'Grass', 'House and 'Sea' regions. This is verified in validation steps. Depending upon this result, the two hidden layer MLP trained with LMBP is taken to be the most suitable network.

In Table 3.14 The best performance given by MLPs of different configurations for 'Grass', 'house' and 'sea' regions with KMC based RoI selection is shown.

In Table 3.15, a summary of the performance of the classifier used to extract RoIs of satellite images are shown in terms of True Positive (TP), True Negative (TN), False Positive (FP), and False Negative (FN).

Table 3.16 shows the comparison of the two proposed methods explained above with two existing methods described in [15] and [104]. Since double hidden layer with hidden neuron number [20 10] and LMBP Training function gives better results, therefore, the results obtained with these combinations are shown here. From the table 3.16 it was seen that the

Table 3.14 Best performance given by MLPs of different configurations for 'Grass', 'house' and 'sea' regions with KMC based RoI selection.

MLP configuration	'Grass' Region		'House' Region		'Sea' region	
	MSE	Time required in Seconds	MSE	Time required in Seconds	MSE	Time required in Seconds
Single hidden layer	0.055	21.39	0.0318	33.51	0.145	27.35
Double hidden layer KMCA	0.0018	88.24	0.0215	90.14	0.0104	81.35
Triple hidden layer	0.0339	193.29	0.0446	180.62	0.0546	137.39

Table 3.15 Summary of classifier performance while extracting RoI of satellite images (shown in terms of True Positive (TP), True Negative (TN), False Positive (FP), and False Negative (FN))

Sl. No.	Type	Average process time in Sec.	TP in %	TN in %	FP in %	FN in %
1.	MLP+manual labeling	90.34	82.6	6.2	5.9	5.3
2.	MLP+KMC	88.24	80.6	8.2	6.3	4.9

Table 3.16 Comparison of the proposed methods with existing methods

Methods	'Grass' Region		'House' Region		'Sea' region		Average Accuracy in %
	MSE	Time required in Seconds	MSE	Time required in Seconds	MSE	Time required in Seconds	
Proposed method	0.0019	90.34	0.0219	92.54	0.0114	82.44	92.17
Proposed method+ KMCA	0.0018	88.24	0.0215	90.14	0.0104	81.35	92.67
S. Arumuga Devi et.al.[15]	0.0189	136.56	0.0345	178.67	0.0235	157.45	90.21
A. Hassanat et.al.[104]	0.0178	156.56	0.0435	189.85	0.0256	169.34	91.23

proposed method described in Section 3.3 gives better results in terms of MSE, accuracy, and time required for computation. For the 'Grass' region the performances of the methods discussed in Section 3.2 and 3.3 and that reported in [15] and [104] are best. The combination of two hidden layer MLP (20,10) and KMC produces MSE of 0.0018 which is 5.5% better than the value obtained with the method discussed in Section 3.2 This is 9.2 times better than that reported in [15] and 8.8 times superior to the results presented in [104]. Similarly, it produces average accuracy of 92.67 which is 2.7% better than that reported in [15] and 1.6% superior to the results presented in [104]. The corresponding improvement in computational time is 54.75% and 77.4%. This indicates the advantage of the proposed approach.

3.4   Conclusion

In this work, two approaches for content extraction of satellite images are presented. In the first method, a simplified ANN-based approach for the segmentation of satellite images in complex backgrounds is proposed. The work considers the formation and training of an ANN in which the pixel values of the various region of the image are used as the target. The method does not require any feature extraction, labeling of objects, region growing or splitting methods to configure and train an ANN, which for the work is an MLP trained with (error) BP learning. As this method requires manual intervention to select the various RoI of the image, a second method is proposed, where the KMC algorithm is used to label the particular RoI in the image, and the region is used as the target to train the MLP. The ANN is trained with different training functions. The network is also trained with the single, double, and triple hidden layers. Then the MSE between the output image and desired images is calculated. From the experimental results it is seen that when trained with LMBP, double hidden layer MLP gives better results for both approaches. The methods are compared with two existing methods which show that the proposed methods give better results. Yet there is a scope for further improvement in MSE convergence and computation time. Further, the image details captured for training the classifiers should have in-depth content. This is necessary to enhance the reliability aspect. Presently, DL-based approaches are preferred for such situations. In the next chapter, a work-related to semantic segmentation of sections of satellite images is reported. The work involves the used DL network ie. CNN.

4

Deep Learning based Semantic

Segmentation Applied to Satellite Images

In this chapter, an approach based on deep learning for semantic segmentation of satellite images is proposed. The method comprises of training and formation of a SegNet which is a DNN. In this case, the inputs are satellite images. In the work, the target to the network has been taken from the output of the algorithm of KMC generating labeled RoI. The RoI is reinforced by the learning of the CNN which is later used

for extraction and identification of required sections from satellite images. From the experimental results, it is seen that the proposed approach performs satisfactorily.[3]

4.1 Introduction

As already discussed, satellite images carry essential information required for a range of applications. Information extraction from satellite images is a challenging issue and requires a host of support. Further automation of information extraction, reliability, and decision-making regarding content is an essential and vital element in a satellite image interpretation system including GIS extraction. To classify different regions in satellite images, semantic segmentation is frequently used. Here each pixel of an image is associated with a class that represents the required RoI [5]. It is essential for many image analysis tasks as it helps in image identification, analysis, processing, and modification. The semantic segmentation differentiates between the objects of interest and their background or other objects. Semantic segmentation is also used in many applications such as autonomous driving, industrial inspection, medical imaging analysis, military reconnaissance, weather forecast, land use patterns, crop census, ocean resources, and groundwater studies, etc. [5].

An ideal algorithm of image segmentation is expected to segment objects which are unknown or new. Several approaches such as semantic texton forest [6] and random forest-based classifiers [7] for semantic segmentation have been reported. Many of these approaches depend on the characteristics of images that can be measured. For this reason, these methods work well in some of the cases and do not work well in others. Again, there are some

[3]A part of this work is reported in [112] and [113].

1. M. Barthakur and K.K. Sarma, Semantic Segmentation using K-means Clustering and Deep Learning in Satellite Image, in Proceedings of 2nd IEEE International Conference on Innovations in Electronics, Signal Processing and Communication (IESC 2019), Shillong, Meghalaya, March, 2019.

2. M. Barthakur and K.K. Sarma, Deep Learning Based Semantic Segmentation Applied to Satellite Image, In Data Visualization and Knowledge Engineering. Lecture Notes on Data Engineering and Communications Technologies, vol 32. Springer, Cham, 2019.

unintentional alterations in the images due to noise, image intensity non-uniformity, missing or occluded portion in the image, etc. Therefore, for segmentation in complex images, methods based on prior knowledge may be more suitable than other approaches. For these reasons, neuro-computing methods with learning algorithms have been applied extensively [8][9][10]. Of late, among the learning-based approaches, deep neural network (DNN) supported methods have been found to be efficient and reliable. These are preferred for semantic segmentation. Most of the semantic segmentation problems are performed using DNN, such as CNNs [9][10][11]. In terms of efficiency and accuracy, these methods are surpassing other methods.

In this chapter, an approach based on DL for semantic segmentation in satellite images is proposed. The method comprises of training and formation of a SegNet where the input images are satellite images. In the work, the target to the network has been taken from the output of the algorithm of KMC with their label of the required RoI generate from the iterations as part of the clustering. The RoI is reinforced by the learning of the CNN which is later used for extraction and identification. Then, with the output of the SegNet as input and the pixel values of various RoI as the target, a neuro-computing structure is trained as a classifier to segment out the various RoIs. Here, the neuro-computing structure is an MLP. The MLP is trained with (error) BP learning.

The proposed method uses raw images as input and has no dependence on hand-crafted features. Further, the approach does not use any pre-processing techniques such as region growing, region split- merge, etc. The method automates the approach of information extraction from satellite images. Raw image inputs are used to configure and train the SegNet, which is a deep CNN with encoder-decoder architecture. It is trained with (error) BP learning. The output of the SegNet is used for classification and decision using the multi-layered neuro- computing classifier, the MLP. From experimental results, it can be concluded the method is appropriate for real-world and reliable.

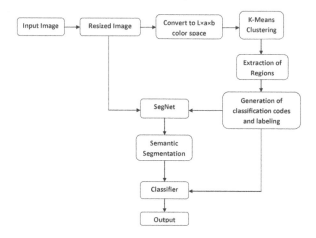

Fig. 4.1 System model of the method

4.2 Proposed Approach

The system model for the proposed work is shown in Fig. 4.1. Each block of the work is described in the following sections.

1. The input in this work is satellite images. The images are taken from United States Geological Survey [102] and deep globe database [108], and image grouping for training, validation, and testing are done as discussed in Section 3.2.

   At first, 50% of the original image is taken as input by resizing it. Then it is converted to $L \times a \times b$ color space. The color space has layers of luminosity 'L', chromaticity 'a', and chromaticity 'b'. The color information can be obtained from 'a' and 'b' layers. Therefore, for further processing, the 'a' and 'b' values of the converted image pixels are used. The other 50% image is used without resizing. It helps to make the system robust though a minor rise in computational complexity is observed.

2. The KMC algorithm is applied to group different similar regions of the image. To group the data so that the similar objects fall on one cluster and dissimilar on the other, KMC algorithm iteration is run over the test and validation images. the KCM is an algorithm that classifies or groups the objects in the image into K different groups. K is a positive number. By minimizing the Euclidean distances between data and its cluster centroid, the grouping is done. Let us consider the image that is to be cluster is of resolution of $x \times y$. Let the input pixel to be cluster be p(x, y) and the cluster centers are c_k. The KCM algorithm is shown in a few steps as below [30]:

Step 1. The cluster number k, and their center be initialized.

Step 2. The Euclidean distance d, between the initialized center and each image pixel be calculated as-

$$d = \| p(x,y) - c_k \| \tag{4.1}$$

Step 3. Based on distance d, to the nearest centers, all pixels in the image be assigned.

Step 4. New position of the center be recalculated after assigning all pixels using the relation given below.

$$c_k = \frac{1}{k} \sum_{y \epsilon c_k} \sum_{x \epsilon c_k} (p(x,y)) \tag{4.2}$$

Step 5. The process be repeated until it achieves minimum error value.

Step 6. Then the pixels in the cluster be reshaped into the image. The index returned by the algorithm corresponds to the clusters in the image. Using these index values, the labeling of every pixel in the image is done. Then the RoI of the image is extracted, according to the labeled pixels.

3. Using the RoI as input and the label image of each RoI as the target, the SegNet [8] is trained with the back-propagation algorithm. SegNet is a deep fully convolutional neural network architecture for semantic pixel-wise segmentation. It has an encoder network and a corresponding decoder network, followed by a final pixel-wise classification layer as shown in Fig. 4.2. The encoder network consists of 13 convolutional layers. Each encoder layer has a corresponding decoder layer and hence the decoder network has 13 layers. The final decoder output is fed to a multi-class softmax classifier to produce class probabilities for each pixel independently. Each encoder in the encoder network performs convolution with a filter bank to produce a set of feature maps. These are then batch normalized [109]. Then an element-wise rectified linear non-linearity (ReLU), (max(0, x)) is applied. Following that, max-pooling with a 2×2 window and stride 2 (non-overlapping window) is performed and the resulting output is sub-sampled by a factor of 2. The max-pooling indices are stored before sub-sampled as these indices are input features containing the boundary information and used in the decoder network. The decoder network upsamples the input feature maps using the memorized max-pooling indices from the corresponding encoder feature map. This step produces sparse feature maps. In the decoder network, the feature maps are convolved with a trainable decoder filter bank to produce dense feature maps. The high dimensional feature representation at the output of the final decoder is fed to a trainable soft-max classifier. This soft-max classifies each pixel independently. The predicted segmentation corresponds to the class with maximum probability at each pixel [110].

4. The output of the SegNet will be an image where each pixel of the image is associated with a class of what is being represented.

5. From the output of the SegNet, the required RoI is selected. The pixel values of the different required regions are taken as the RoI. To segment, the sea region pixel values

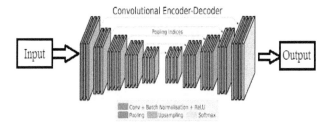

Fig. 4.2 SegNet Architecture [8]

of that region are kept as it is and other values are kept as 0. Thus the pixel values of a particular region will be the target for the classifier to segment out the region.

6. With the output of the SegNet as input and the pixel values of various RoI as the target, a neuro-computing structure is trained to segment the various RoI. Here the neuro-computing structure is an MLP. The MLP is trained with (error) BP algorithm and used as the classifier at the last end. To learn applied patterns, the classifier is configured. The process through which the classifier learns is called training. The classifier is trained with the BP algorithm. Depending on the BP algorithm, the weights between the layers of the classifier are updated. Till the performance results meet their goal, this adaptive updating of the classifier is continued.

The process map for the work is shown in Fig. 4.3. Here, the feature map obtained as SegNet output is used to train a feed-forward classifier with the labeled RoI as the target.

4.3   Results and Discussion

The experimental results are discussed in the following sections. In Section 5.3.1 the results obtained for the SegNet network are discussed. The results obtained from the classifier are discussed in Section 5.3.2.

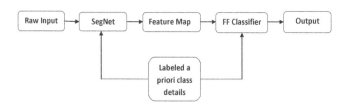

Fig. 4.3 The process map for the proposed work

4.3.1   Results obtained from SegNet

The method is tested using a set of samples out of which two images- "Satellite image 1" and "Satellite image 2" are taken for discussion. The two example images used for testing are shown in Fig.s 4.4 and 4.7. These images are used to segment the "grass", "house" and "sea" area of the image. The regions such as "grass" region, "house" region, and "sea" region obtained from the KCM algorithm for the "Satellite image 1" are shown in Fig. 4.5. Similarly, the regions such as "grass" region, "house" region, and "sea" region obtained from the KCM algorithm for the "Satellite image 2" are shown in Fig. 4.8. The SegNet is trained with the input images and with the RoI obtained from the KCM algorithm and its label images. In the SegNet, 4 encoder network and 4 decoder network is used. The convolution and deconvolution filter size is kept fixed to 3×3. The bias term in all convolutional layers is fixed to zero. A detailed description of the encoder-decoder layers is shown in Table 4.1. From Table 4.1 it is seen that the input to the SegNet is of size $350 \times 467 \times 3$. The encoder1 performs convolution with 64 filters of size 3×3 with zero padding 1 and stride 1. The size of the output of the convolution layer is $350 \times 467 \times 64$. Then batch normalization is done on the convolution layer output [109]. After that element-wise ReLU operation, (max $(0, x)$) is performed. Following that, max-pooling with a non-overlapping window of size 2×2 and stride 2 is performed. The size of the output of max-pooling is $175 \times 233 \times 64$.

Then in encoder2 convolution with 64 filters of size 3×3 with zero padding 1 and stride 1 is performed. The size of the output of the convolution layer is $175 \times 233 \times 64$. Then batch normalization is done. After that ReLU operation, (max $(0, x)$) is performed. Then max-pooling with a non-overlapping window of size 2×2 and stride 2 is performed. The size of the output of max-pooling is $87 \times 116 \times 64$. Then encoder3 performs convolution using the same filter size as in encoder 2 and encoder 3. The size of the output of the convolution layer in encoder3 is $87 \times 116 \times 64$. Then again batch normalization is performed. After that again element-wise ReLU operation performed. Then max-pooling is performed. Now, the size of the output of max-pooling is $43 \times 58 \times 64$. Then in encoder4, the same operations are repeated. The size of the output in the convolution layer is $43 \times 58 \times 64$ and max-pooling is $21 \times 29 \times 64$. The indices of max-pooling are recorded in each encoder and used in the decoder network. The decoder network upsamples the input feature maps using the stored max-pooling indices which are recorded in each encoder network. From the Table 4.1, the size of the input to the decoder4 is $21 \times 29 \times 64$. These feature maps are then upsampled and the size after unpooling is $43 \times 58 \times 64$. Then deconvolution is performed with 64 filters of size 3×3 with zero padding 1 and stride 1. The output size in this step is $43 \times 58 \times 64$. Then ReLU and batch normalization are performed. Further in decoder3, the feature maps are upsampled and the size after unpooling is $87 \times 116 \times 64$. Then deconvolution is performed with 64 filters of size 3×3 with zero padding 1 and stride 1. The output size in this step is $87 \times 116 \times 64$. Next, ReLU and batch normalization are performed. In decoder2 again upsampling, deconvolution, batch normalization, and ReLU are carried out. The size after upsampling and deconvolution turns out to be $175 \times 233 \times 64$. After upsampling and deconvolution, the size of output becomes $350 \times 467 \times 64$. Finally, the output of the final decoder is fed to a soft-max classifier that has been trained. This soft-max classifies each pixel independently. The predicted segmentation of the softmax is the class with maximum probability at each pixel. The weights of the Convolution layers

Fig. 4.4 Input for "Satellite image 1"

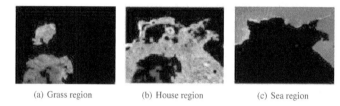

(a) Grass region   (b) House region   (c) Sea region

Fig. 4.5 RoIs obtained from k-means algorithm for "satellite image 1".

in the encoder and decoder sub-networks are initialized using the Microsoft Research Asia

(MSRA) weight initialization method. The output of the proposed method is shown in Fig.s

4.6 and 4.9. The method is also compared with the results of existing methods SegNet [8]

and DeepLab-v2 [111]. The accuracy of the method is also compared by increasing the depth

of the encoder to 6 and 8. The workflow of the SegNet architecture is shown in Fig. 4.10.

Table 4.1 A detailed description of the encoder-decoder layer specifications of the SegNet
used for the proposed work

Encoder block			Output size		Decoder block		Output size
Input	Image Input	$350 \times 467 \times 3$ with 'zerocenter' normalization.		Output	Pixel Classification Layer	Cross-entropy loss with 'sea','house', and 1 other classes	
					Softmax	Softmax	
Encoder 1	Convolution	64 3 convolution	$350 \times 467 \times 64$	Decoder 1	Convolution	64 3 convolution	$350 \times 467 \times 64$

		with padding 1 and stride 1					with padding 1 and stride 1	
	Batch Normalization	Batch Normalization with 64 channels				Batch Normalization	Batch Normalization with 64 channels	
	ReLU	ReLU				ReLU	ReLU	
	Convolution	64 3 convolution with padding 1 and stride 1	350 × 467 × 64			Convolution	64 3 convolution with padding 1 and stride 1	350 × 467 × 64
	Batch Normalization	Batch Normalization with 64 channels				Batch Normalization	Batch Normalization with 64 channels	
	ReLU	ReLU				ReLU	ReLU	
	Max Pooling	2 × 2 max pooling with stride 2 and padding 0	175 × 233 × 64			Max Unpooling	Max Unpooling	350 × 467 × 64
Encoder 2	Convolution	64 3 convolution with padding 1 and stride 1	175 × 233 × 64		Decoder 2	Convolution	64 3 convolution with padding 1 and stride 1	175 × 233 × 64
	Batch Normalization	Batch Normalization with 64 channels				Batch Normalization	Batch Normalization with 64 channels	
	ReLU	ReLU				ReLU	ReLU	
	Convolution	64 3 convolution with padding 1 and stride 1	175 × 233 × 64			Convolution	64 3 convolution with padding 1 and stride 1	175 × 233 × 64
	Batch Normalization	Batch Normalization with 64 channels				Batch Normalization	Batch Normalization with 64 channels	
	ReLU	ReLU				ReLU	ReLU	
	Max Pooling	2 × 2 max pooling with stride 2 and padding 0	87 × 116 × 64			Max Unpooling	Max Unpooling	175 × 233 × 64
Encoder 3	Convolution	64 3	87 × 116 × 64		Decoder 2	Convolution	64 3	87 × 116 × 64

		convolution with padding 1 and stride 1				convolution with padding 1 and stride 1	
	Batch Normalization	Batch Normalization with 64 channels			Batch Normalization	Batch Normalization with 64 channels	
	ReLU	ReLU			ReLU	ReLU	
	Convolution	64 3 convolution with padding 1 and stride 1	87 × 116 × 64		Convolution	64 3 convolution with padding 1 and stride 1	87 × 116 × 64
	Batch Normalization	Batch Normalization with 64 channels			Batch Normalization	Batch Normalization with 64 channels	
	ReLU	ReLU			ReLU	ReLU	
	Max Pooling	2 × 2 max pooling with stride 2 and padding 0	45 × 58 × 64		Max Unpooling	Max Unpooling	87 × 116 × 64
Encoder 4	Convolution	64 3 convolution with padding 1 and stride 1	45 × 58 × 64	Decoder 4	Convolution	64 3 convolution with padding 1 and stride 1	45 × 58 × 64
	Batch Normalization	Batch Normalization with 64 channels			Batch Normalization	Batch Normalization with 64 channels	
	ReLU	ReLU			ReLU	ReLU	
	Convolution	64 3 convolution with padding 1 and stride 1	45 × 58 × 64		Convolution	64 3 convolution with padding 1 and stride 1	45 × 58 × 64
	Batch Normalization	Batch Normalization with 64 channels			Batch Normalization	Batch Normalization with 64 channels	
	ReLU	ReLU			ReLU	ReLU	
	Max Pooling	2 × 2 max pooling with stride 2 and padding 0	21 × 29 × 64		Max Unpooling	Max Unpooling	45 × 58 × 64

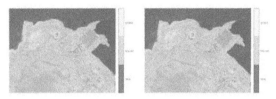

(a) Output obtained from SegNet (b) SegNet output when trained with
when trained with "Satellite image 1"   "Satellite image 1" and its label im-
and its RoI obtained from k-means age
algorithm

Fig. 4.6 Output images

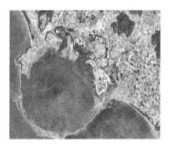

Fig. 4.7 Example of Input image, "Satellite image 2"

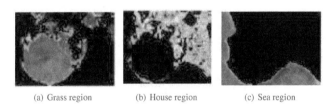

(a) Grass region   (b) House region   (c) Sea region

Fig. 4.8 RoI obtained from k-means algorithm for "satellite image 2"

Table 4.2 Experimental results for "satellite image 1"

Images	Accuracy	Mean IoU	Weighted IoU	BF-score
Proposed method (Segnet+KMCA)	94.35%	66.77%	88.29%	60.35%
SegNet [8]	93.26%	64.42%	86.84%	59.65%
DeepLab-v2 [55]	93.56%	66.67%	87.65%	59.21%

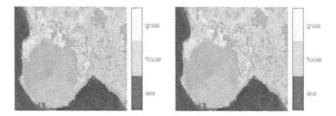

(a) Output obtained from proposed method (b) SegNet output when trained with "Satel-
when trained with "Satellite image 2" and its lite image 2" and its label image
RoI obtained from k-means algorithm

Fig. 4.9 Output images for "Satellite image 2"

Table 4.3 Experimental results for "satellite image 2"

Images	Accuracy	Mean IoU	Weighted IoU	BF-score
Proposed method (Segnet+KMCA)	92.63%	61.64%	87.86%	59.84%
SegNet [8]	92.45%	60.32%	86.43%	58.24%
DeepLab-v2 [55]	92.56%	60.67%	86.65%	58.16%

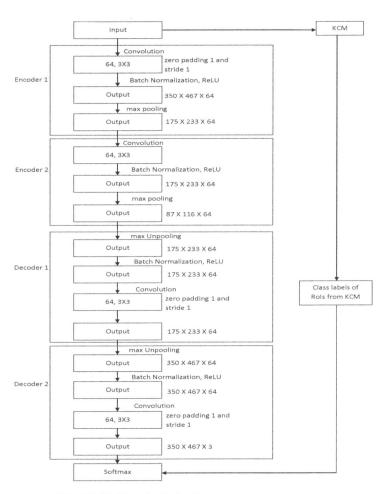

Fig. 4.10 Workflow for the SegNet

Table 4.4 Experimental results when depth of encoder is increased for "satellite image 1"

Method	Encoder depth	Accuracy
The proposed method	4	94.35%
	6	95.47%
	8	95.93%

Table 4.5 Experimental results when depth of encoder is increased for "satellite image 2"

Method	Encoder depth	Accuracy
The proposed method	4	92.63%
	6	92.88%
	8	93.43%

Table 4.2 shows the experimental results obtained for "Satellite image 1". It is seen that the accuracy is 94.35% for the proposed method and that for the SegNet and DeepLab-v2 are 93.26% and 93.56% respectively. Again the mean IoU is 66.77% for the proposed method and that for the SegNet and DeepLab-v2 are 64.42% and 66.67% respectively and the weighted IoU is 88.29% for the proposed method and that for the SegNet and DeepLab-v2 are 86.84% and 87.65% respectively. Finally, the BF-score 60.35% for the proposed method and that for the SegNet and DeepLab-v2 are 59.65% and 59.21% respectively. The result obtained from the proposed method is better with 94.35% accuracy.

Table 4.3 shows the experimental results obtained for "Satellite image 2". It is seen that the accuracy is 92.63% for the proposed method and that for the SegNet and DeepLab-v2 are 92.45% and 92.56% respectively. Again the mean IoU is 61.64% for the proposed method and that for the SegNet and DeepLab-v2 are 60.32% and 60.67% respectively and the weighted IoU is 87.86% for the proposed method and that for the SegNet and DeepLab-v2 are 86.43% and 86.65% respectively. Finally, the BF-score 59.84% for the proposed method and that for the SegNet and DeepLab-v2 are 58.24% and 58.16% respectively. Thus for both images, the proposed method gives better results.

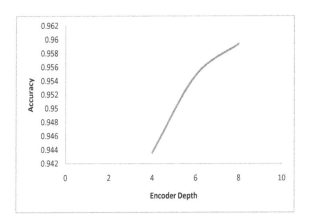

Fig. 4.11 Encoder depth Vs Accuracy plot for "satellite image 1"

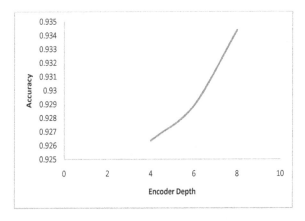

Fig. 4.12 Encoder depth Vs Accuracy plot for "satellite image 2"

Table 4.4 and 4.5 show how the accuracy of the method changes with the increase in encoder depth. It was seen that when the depth of the encoder increases accuracy is also increases. In Fig.s 4.11 and 4.12 show encoder depth versus accuracy for two samples. Fig. 4.13 shows the normalized confusion matrix for the proposed method when trained with "satellite image 1". It is seen that 97.75 % of the sea region, 98.61% of the house region, and 87.25% of the grass region are predicted correctly. Thus the sea and the house region are predicted properly than the grass region. In Fig. 4.14 the normalized confusion matrix for "satellite image 1" when trained with SegNet is shown. It is seen that 96.65% of the sea region, 99.61% of the house region, and 86.25 % of the grass region are predicted correctly by the SegNet method. Thus when compared the two normalized confusion matrix, it is seen that the prediction result for sea and grass region in the proposed method is better than the SegNet method reported in [8]

Fig. 4.15 shows the training progress plot of the SegNet after 6150. It shows that the training stabilizes after 3000 epochs.

4.3.2   Experimental results for the classifier

With the output of the SegNet as input and the pixel values of various RoI as the target, a neuro-computing structure is trained to segment the various RoI. Here, the neuro-computing structure is an MLP. The MLP is trained with the BP algorithm. At first, five different training functions are used to train the classifier. Then, between the classifier output and target image, MSE had been calculated for all the training functions and both "satellite image 1" and "satellite image 2" the images. The experimental results are shown in Table 4.6 when trained for the "Sea" region. The classifier network forms of BP namely LMBP, CGBP, SGBP, BRBP, and RBP algorithms. The relevant details of these versions of BP have been mentioned in Chapter 2. It has been seen that the training function LMBP is the fastest learning algorithm. As mentioned already MLPs are trained with single, double, and triple hidden layers with

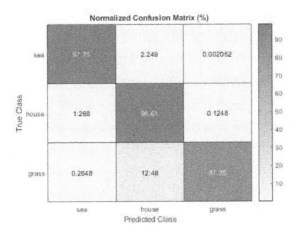

Fig. 4.13 Confusion matrix for the proposed method

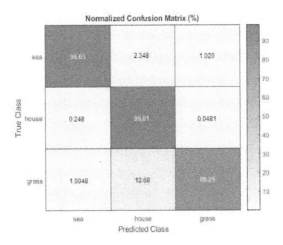

Fig. 4.14 Confusion matrix for SegNet

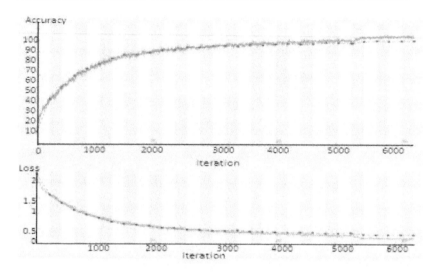

Fig. 4.15 Training progress plot with 6150 epoch and maximum iteration 6150.

different numbers of hidden neurons. Here the training function used is LMBP as it is the fastest (proven from experiments). Then again, MSE between the classifier output and target image is calculated. In Table 4.7, the results are shown when trained for the "Sea" region. It is seen that the double hidden layer case of MLP trained with LMBP gives better results than single and triple hidden layered configuration. This indicates better learning and feature capture by the double-layered MLP (with neuron numbers 20 and 10 (Table 4.8)). It requires 101.64 seconds to train and an MSE convergence of 0.0016 is generated. In Fig.s 4.16 and 4.17, the outputs of the classifier are shown.

From Table 4.6 when trained for "Grass" region of "Satellite image 1", it is seen that with LMBP, the MLP produces the best MSE of 0.0068 in 24.68 seconds, SCG gives MSE of 0.0417 in 174.32 seconds, CGBP gives MSE of 0.0649 in 271.45 seconds, BRBP gives MSE of 0.0417 in 53.64 seconds and RBP gives MSE of 0.0936 in 571.41 seconds.

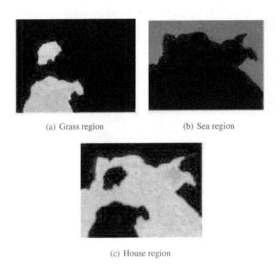

(a) Grass region   (b) Sea region

(c) House region

Fig. 4.16 Classifier output for "Satellite image 1"

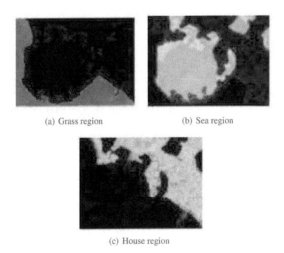

(a) Grass region   (b) Sea region

(c) House region

Fig. 4.17 Classifier output for "Satellite image 2"

Table 4.6 Experimental results for the "Grass" region of "Satellite image 1" when trained with different training functions.

Methods	No. of Hidden Neuron	Time required in seconds	MSE
Levenberg- Marquardt Back-propagation	10	22.69	0.0448
	20	24.68	0.0068
	30	27.87	0.0075
	40	34.99	0.0083
	50	36.79	0.0090
	60	38.74	0.0158
	70	42.83	0.0241
	80	48.51	0.0321
	90	51.32	0.0480
	100	53.77	0.0593
Scaled conjugate Gradient	10	111.69	0.0627
	20	174.32	0.0417
	30	194.22	0.0536
	40	212.46	0.0624
	50	257.22	0.0736
	60	293.63	0.0802

	70	326.52	0.0834
	80	354.22	0.0925
	90	404.19	0.1069
	100	423.66	0.1278
Conjugate Gradient back-propagation with polak-ribiere updates	10	172.34	0.0746
	20	271.45	0.0649
	30	323.46	0.0690
	40	405.63	0.0743
	50	463.45	0.0785
	60	469.25	0.0806
	70	475.11	0.0858
	80	485.44	0.0902
	90	498.45	0.0936
	100	513.33	0.0976
Bayesian Regulation back-propagation	10	49.12	0.0511
	20	53.64	0.0417
	30	58.32	0.0463
	40	62.57	0.0508
	50	66.72	0.0573
	60	69.22	0.0686
	70	72.36	0.0708

	80	74.35	0.0757
	90	78.42	0.0834
	100	79.32	0.0998
Resilient back-propagation	10	571.41	0.0936
	20	576.58	0.0978
	30	590.22	0.0986
	40	597.28	0.1013
	50	612.32	0.1058
	60	616.45	0.1064
	70	619.52	0.1086
	80	622.12	0.1107
	90	625.24	0.1146
	100	627.42	0.1163

From Table 4.7 it is seen that when trained with the "Grass" region of "satellite image 1",
the best MSE for single hidden layer MLP is 0.0068 in 24.68 seconds, for the double hidden
layer is 0.0016 in 101.64 seconds, and for three hidden layers is 207.19 in 0.0351 seconds.

Table 4.7 Experimental results for the "Grass" region of "satellite image 1" when trained
with single, double and triple hidden layer.

ANN with different size of hidden layer	No. of Hidden Neuron	Time required in	MSE

		seconds	
ANN with single hidden layer	10	22.69	0.0448
	20	24.68	0.0068
	30	27.87	0.0075
	40	34.99	0.0083
	50	36.79	0.0090
	60	38.74	0.0158
	70	42.83	0.0241
	80	48.51	0.0321
	90	51.32	0.0480
	100	53.77	0.0593
ANN with double hidden layer	[10 10]	68.34	0.0124
	[10 20]	72.49	0.0121
	[10 30]	75.34	0.0145
	[10 40]	80.23	0.0134
	[10 50]	83.35	0.0135
	[10 60]	85.31	0.0155
	[10 70]	89.32	0.0166
	[10 80]	92.54	0.0169
	[10 90]	96.46	0.0175
	[10 100]	99.44	0.0179

	[20 10]	101.64	0.0016
	[20 20]	104.64	0.0019
	[20 30]	107.76	0.0022
	[20 40]	110.42	0.0024
	[20 50]	119.43	0.0025
	[20 60]	124.44	0.0033
	[20 70]	125.56	0.0039
	[20 80]	128.46	0.0045
	[20 90]	129.46	0.0053
	[20 100]	136.35	0.0069
	[30 10]	137.34	0.0078
	[30 20]	142.16	0.0083
	[30 30]	145.35	0.0095
	[30 40]	153.43	0.00104
	[30 50]	169.33	0.0112
ANN with triple hidden layer	[10 10 10]	207.19	0.0351
	[10 10 20]	225.55	0.0355
	[10 10 30]	235.65	0.0375
	[10 10 40]	247.65	0.0383
	[10 10 50]	269.67	0.0386
	[10 20 10]	265.35	0.0419

[10 20 20]	282.45	0.0436
[10 20 30]	284.45	0.0445
[10 20 40]	286.34	0.0455
[10 20 50]	287.22	0.0474
[10 30 10]	294.31	0.0482
[10 30 20]	298.33	0.0483
[10 30 30]	301.34	0.0496
[10 30 40]	316.42	0.0503
[10 30 50]	322.47	0.0516
[20 10 10]	332.34	0.0526
[20 10 20]	343.22	0.0536
[20 10 30]	355.55	0.0547
[20 10 40]	358.35	0.0552
[20 10 50]	359.12	0.0567
[20 20 10]	363.35	0.0581
[20 20 20]	365.34	0.0593
[20 20 30]	371.39	0.0613
[20 20 40]	373.34	0.0635

At first, the classifier is trained using training functions such as LMBP, SCG, CGBP, BRBP, and RBP training functions. The hidden layer neuron numbers are gradually increased

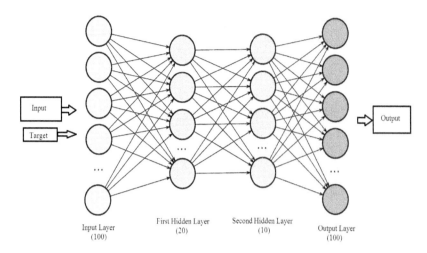

Fig. 4.18 Architecture of the MLP with double hidden layer

from 10 to 100. The results obtained are shown in Table 4.6. It was seen that in terms of the MSE LMBP algorithm shows the better output. MSE is around 0.0068 when hidden neuron number 20. The MSE value calculated for the other training functions is much higher than LM Back-propagation. Subsequently, as LMBP has been established to be the fastest, it is used to train single, double, and triple hidden layer MLP for 'Grass', 'House' and 'Sea' regions as shown in Table 4.7. From the tables, the double hidden layer shows better MSE values than the triple hidden layer and single hidden layer. For "Satellite image 1" the MSE for the double hidden layer was around 0.0016 when the number of hidden neurons is taken as [20 10] which is the best result. In Table 4.8, a summary of the performance of the classifier used to extract RoIs of satellite images are shown in terms of True Positive (TP), True Negative (TN), False Positive (FP), and False Negative (FN). The architecture of MLP with a double hidden layer is shown in Fig. 4.18.

Table 4.9 shows the comparison of the proposed methods explained in Chapter 3 and Chapter 4 with two existing methods described in [15] and [104]. Since double hidden

Table 4.8 Summary of classifier performance while extracting RoI of satellite images (shown in terms of True Positive (TP), True Negative (TN), False Positive (FP), and False Negative (FN))

Sl. No.	Type	Average process time in Sec.	TP in %	TN in %	FP in %	FN in %
1.	MLP	126.24	84.6	6.2	5.0	4.2
2.	Softmax	101.54	83.4	8.2	5.6	2.8

Table 4.9 Comparison of the proposed method with existing methods

Methods	'Grass' Region		'House' Region		'Sea' region		Average % Accuracy
	MSE	Time required in Seconds	MSE	Time required in Seconds	MSE	Time required in Seconds	
Proposed method	0.0019	90.34	0.0219	92.54	0.0114	82.44	92.17
Proposed method+ KMCA	0.0018	88.24	0.0215	90.14	0.0104	81.35	92.67
Proposed method+ SegNeT	0.0016	101.64	0.0213	150.67	0.0098	147.67	93.28
S. Arumuga Devi et.al.[15]	0.0189	136.56	0.0345	178.67	0.0235	157.45	90.21
A. Hassanat et.al.[104]	0.0178	156.56	0.0435	189.85	0.0256	169.34	91.23

layer with hidden neuron number [20 10] and LMBP Training function gives better results, therefore, the results obtained with these combinations are shown here. From the table 4.9 it was seen that the proposed method described in Chapter 4 gives better results both in terms of MSE and time required for computation. For the 'Grass' region the performances of the methods discussed in Section 3.2 and 3.3 and Section 4.2 and that reported in [15] and [104] are best. The combination of two hidden layer MLP (20,10) and SegNet produces an MSE of 0.0016 which is 12.5% better than the value obtained with the method discussed in Section 3.3. This is 10.8 times better than that reported in [15] and 10.12 times superior to the results presented in [104]. The corresponding improvement in computational time is 34.35% and 54.03%. This indicates the advantage of the proposed approach.

4.4   Conclusion

In the chapter, a method for semantic segmentation based on DL in satellite images is proposed. The proposed method comprises the training and formation of a SegNet where the input images are satellite images. In the work, the target to the network has been taken from the output of the KMC algorithm with their label of the required RoI. Then, with the output of the SegNet as input and the pixel values of various RoI as the target, a neuro-computing structure is trained to segment the various RoI. Here an MLP and a soft-max layer are used as the classifiers which are trained with the BP algorithm. The approach does not use any pre-processing techniques such as region growing, region split- merge, etc. to configure and train the SegNet, which is a deep convolutional network and comprises of encoder-decoder structure and the classifier. The method has been tested with different satellite images. The experimental results for both SegNet DNN and the classifier are analyzed. From the experimental results, it has been seen that the method is appropriate for real-world applications and is reliable. Though DL-based models give better results, these models require a lot of training samples for training, otherwise, it leads to over or underfitting. In the case of satellite images, limited data is a common problem as the collection of such images is either expensive or time demanding. Therefore to overcome these problems a semi-supervised adversarial network-based work has been carried out which is reported in the next chapter.

5

Semi Supervised Adversarial Deep
Network for Satellite Images

In Chapter 4, the method based on SegNet DNN, KMC, and learning-based classifier proved to be reliable. But it has a distinct data dependence. In specific situations, relevant data may not be available and may affect RoI labeling. In such a situation, a semi-supervised adversarial network-based approach is appropriate. Such a work is reported in this chapter.[4]

---

[4]A part of this work is published in

5.1   Introduction

The application of learning-aided tools in remote sensing [113][10] technology has proven to

be a boon in terms of quality and reliability. The images extracted from satellite captures are

desired to be of high resolution and should be distortion-free to the widest extent possible.

Many characteristics that are associated with nature are observed to be embedded in high-

resolution satellite images giving finer details of color, shape, texture, structure, and density

[113]. These information exhibits of satellite images are useful in many real-life applications

such as flood prediction, deforestation, weather prediction, land cover mapping, etc. which

have considerable societal impact. In these applications, the extraction of differently textured

regions from a satellite image is an important and crucial task. To extract different regions

from satellite images, researchers have developed a plethora of image segmentation methods.

However, these methods may not work in all high-resolution satellite images as it is very

difficult to know about the texture of different regions in a satellite image. Therefore, when

dealing with such images, prior knowledge-based methods are useful and necessary to carry

out the segmentation process properly. In this backdrop, the importance of learning aided or

artificial intelligence (AI) based tools come to the forefront.

    During the last few decades, learning aided or AI-based approaches have been adopted

for satellite image analysis and content extraction. Lately, the shift has been towards the use

of deep learning which is now the omnipresent approach for the development of learning

aided or AI-based techniques. Many deep learning-based methods and architectures for

image segmentation are available in the literature which adopts prior knowledge as a means

of content extraction in computer vision domains. AlexNet [10], VGG-16 [114], ResNet [55],

Recurrent Convolutional Neural Networks (RCNN) [116] etc. are such architectures that

have achieved significant milestones in semantic segmentation of images. Most of the other

---

1. M. Barthakur, K. K. Sarma and N. Mastorakis, "Modified Semi-Supervised Adversarial Deep Network and Classifier Combination for Segmentation of Satellite Images," in IEEE Access, vol. 8, pp. 117972-117985, 2020. **(Impact Factor-3.745)**

state-of-the-art algorithms are based on these approaches. For example, in [127] and [128] the authors used Convolutional Neural Networks (CNN) based framework for hyperspectral image (HSI) analysis. Similarly, in [60] the authors presented an algorithm for semantic segmentation of slums in satellite images using transfer learning on fully convolutional neural networks.

Although deep learning-based methods produce an efficient performance for semantic image segmentation, the models usually have a serious problem which is known as overfitting [45][12]. Overfitting occurs when a deep learning-based model learns the details more than required. Further, the noise present in the training data to a limited degree negatively impacts the performance of the model when implemented on new data [13]. The reason behind the problem is that a huge number of learnable parameters need to be trained by these methods and therefore, a large volume of data for training is required. The problem of overfitting becomes severe if limited training data are used. For high-resolution satellite images, limited training data is a familiar problem as the collection of such images is either expensive or time-consuming. Therefore, effective and new strategies for training deep learning-based models are required to overcome the problem of overfitting. The use of the Generative Adversarial Network (GAN) [129] has been verified to be effective in reducing overfitting during training. The GAN consists of two networks- generative (G) and discriminative (D) [129]. The GAN is trained with the adversarial algorithm. The main objective of G is to generate samples as the target data, as close to the real ones as possible. Next, D attempts to separate the generated samples from the targets. Since the two networks are trained through back-propagation (BP), the G and D emerge to be better in their assignments after each training iteration. Thus, through adversarial training, the problem of overfitting can be eliminated, even if limited numbers of training samples are used. Several applications [117],[118],[119],[120] have used adversarial training approaches where most of the methods are semi-supervised which can tackle the problem of the limited number of training samples. Semi-supervised methods for adversarial training are also useful in other applications such as object detection, medical image analysis, etc. In [130], an object detection method, based on weakly-supervised and high-level feature learning has been discussed. Similarly, in [131] a method for anomaly detection based on semi-supervised adversarial training has been presented. Again in [132], object detection has been carried out with semi-annotated weak labels. These applications also demonstrate the ability to overcome the problem of limited data.

From the above discussion, it is obvious that deep networks require a lot of training and annotated data. In the case of content extraction of satellite images, each pixel of training images must be annotated, which is difficult to perform for all cases. Again, unsupervised learning methods have not been very successful for the extraction of regions in satellite images because they lack the concept of classes and merely attempted to identify consistent regions [121] based on certain similarities. Hence, there is a scope to use a combination of unsupervised training and labeled data to process applied inputs to generate reliable classification. The algorithm in [120] uses two networks (segmentation and discriminator) which are trained adversarially for semantic segmentation of natural images. The method in [120] mainly aims to design a fully convolutional discriminator network. In addition to that, in the algorithm, supervisory signals from trustworthy regions of predicted unlabeled images are provided for proper training of the segmentation network.

In contrast to that, the work reported here discusses the methodology, experiments, and results related to attempts made to extract different regions from satellite images where two networks for segmentation and discriminator are used with the semi-supervised adversarial algorithm to get the semantic labels of different regions in the images. The outputs of the segmentation network are the probability maps of the semantic labels of the given satellite images used as measures to ascertain the quality of the training which is required in subsequent cycles. The confidence map is used to calculate the semi-supervised loss. The semi-supervised loss is again used to train the segmentation network when unlabeled input images are used as input. The segmentation network aims to minimize this loss. Further, in this work, a semi-supervised adversarial learning method with architectural expansion and several other additions is presented which is used to extract different regions of interest (RoIs) such as Forest Land, Agriculture Land, Rangeland, Urban Land, Barren Land, Water, etc. from satellite images. In the proposed approach, in addition to unlabeled data, some supervision is also applied during training. Though the algorithm for semi-supervised adversarial learning reported in [120] has been adopted for this work to get the semantic labels of different regions in the satellite images, significant changes as discussed below have been made in the architecture and feeding mechanism to derive enhanced performance and reliability.

The discriminator network is fully convolutional with structural (use of extended layers), parametric, and configuration modification. The modifications include variation in convolutional filter masks, stride, activation functions, learning rate, gradient descent, and mean square error (MSE) convergence goal, all of which are different compared to that in the network used in [120]. The output of the discriminator network is called the confidence map which is a spatial probability map whose pixel values represent whether it is sampled from the ground truth map or the predicted map of the segmentation network. Again, the goal of the segmentation network is to fool the discriminator network i.e., it generates images in such a way so that the discriminator network cannot differentiate between the ground truth and the images generated by the segmentation network and better output from the segmentation network is achieved. In this process, with the help of cross-entropy loss linked to the segmentation network and the ground truth label maps, and the adversarial loss linked to the discriminator network, the segmentation network is trained to produce better outputs that are close to ground truth label maps. For the unlabeled images, along with the adversarial loss, the semi-supervised loss linked to the confidence maps generated by the discriminator is used as a supervisory signal to predict outputs of the segmentation network so that the generated outputs are as close as possible to the ground truth. After that, the outputs of the segmentation network, which are the semantic labels of RoIs of satellite images, are used as input to train a number of classifiers out of which the best one is selected to extract and separate the RoIs of the satellite image from the semantic labels. The classifiers are used to provide better reliability during segmentation through accurate identification of the extracted sections from the satellite image.

A total of seven classifiers such as Multi-layer Perceptron (MLP), Fuzzy C-means (FCM), Softmax classifier, Support Vector Machine (SVM), K-nearest neighbor (KNN), Self Organizing Map (SOM), and Probabilistic Neural Network (PNN) are used for ascertaining the most suitable one. Further, the results obtained from each of the classifiers are compared to formulate a reliable combination. The target to the classifiers is the required RoIs which are selected from the ground truth label images by setting the pixel values of RoIs as 1 and others as 0. To validate the proposed method, it has been tested with DeepGlobe Land Cover Classification Challenge dataset [108].

Further, the proposed work has been tested with four different input feeding mechanisms that include delayed feed with data augmentation, use of noise removal and edge sharpening filters, and scrambled input with the assumption of obtaining better performance.

5.2 Proposed Method

In this section, the proposed approach is discussed. The description includes the architecture of the system, learning schemes adopted, and methodology of training and testing. In this work, semi-supervised training with adversarial learning with architectural expansion and certain modifications as discussed above is used (Fig. 5.1).

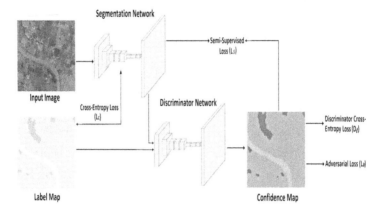

Fig. 5.1 The block diagram for semi supervised training with adversarial network

5.2.1 Architecture of the network

The architecture of the proposed approach consists of segmentation and discriminator networks. The segmentation network is designed for semantic segmentation and the discriminator network helps to get better and reliable output from the segmentation network. The four input feeding mechanisms using which the method is tested to obtain better results are discussed below.

Further, a total of seven classifiers are used to extract the RoIs from the satellite images. Subsequently, the results of each of the classifiers namely MLP, FCM, Softmax, SVM, KNN, SOM, and PNN are compared and the most suitable one for the discrimination of the RoIs ascertained. These are also discussed in this section.

Input feeding mechanism

Variation in input feed and diversity in data assist learning in deep neural networks (DNN). Further, to optimize the quality of input data which also adds to the volume of dataset, diversity, content richness, and help in better evaluation and analysis of the network performances

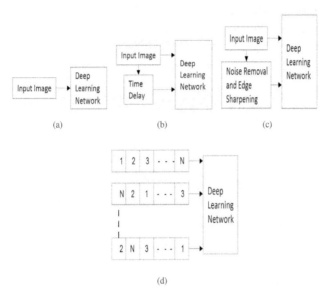

Fig. 5.2 Input feeding mechanisms (a) Direct feeding of input (b) Feeding of input images for sample augmentation with time delay (c) Feeding of input images with noise removal, edge sharpening (d) Scrambled input feed

and output quality, modifications and structural expansions have been made in DNNs [133]. Four methods for feeding the input into the network have been used in this work. These are 1) Direct feeding of input, 2) Feeding of input images with time delay for sample augmentation, 3) Feeding of input images with noise removal and edge sharpening, and 4) Scrambled input feed. These methods are discussed below.

Direct feeding of input   In this method, the satellite images are fed into the network without any pre-processing (Fig. 5.2(a)). The raw data is used to learn the regions and carry out the related processes. The advantage is that the content is in the intrinsic format and the learning obtains the most naturally relevant details.

Feeding of input images with time delay for sample augmentation   Some data augmentation methods such as flipping the image vertically and horizontally and rotating the image by an angle of 50 degrees are applied to the images to produce diversity in the images. Then after feeding the original images into the network, the augmented images are fed into the network through a time delay line (Fig. 5.2(b)). This method of feeding input into the network increases the correlation between the input image contents and helps in augmented learning.

Feeding of input images with noise removal, edge sharpening   In this method, at first Gaussian low pass filter is applied to the images to remove any noise which may be acquired during image capture. Next, a Gaussian high pass filter is applied to sharpen the images. At this point, the original and filtered images are fed into the network (Fig. 5.2(c)).

Scrambled input feed   The feeding sequence of the inputs is varied and the learning cycles are repeated (Fig. 5.2(d)). This helps the network to learn all the patterns in much greater detail and make discrimination despite variations in the feeding sequence. It enables the network to deal with realistic variations that are encountered in practical situations.

Segmentation Network

In this work, the Deeplab-v2 [122] framework with ResNet-101 [55] model has been adopted as the segmentation network [120]. The strides of the last two convolutional layers are modified from 2 to 1 and the last classification layer is removed to make the output feature map resolution effective for 12.5% (1/8) amount of the input image size. The dilated convolution has been applied [123] in *conv*4 and *conv*5 layers with 2 and 4 strides respectively to enlarge the receptive fields. An up-sampling layer with the *softmax* layer is applied finally, to match the input image size. These are done to check the robustness of the proposed approach.

Discriminator Network

The discriminator is a fully convolutional network [120] where the number of convolution layer is modified to 4 with 3×3 kernel and $\{68, 128, 256, 1\}$ channels with the stride of 1 to reduce the dimension of the network. This is primarily due to the fact that the network is configured to discriminate only seven regions which are to be extracted from the satellite images. Leaky- ReLU [123] with 0.2 parameter after each convolutional layer is used. Finally, an up-sampling layer is taken into consideration as the final layer of the network so that the dimension of the output matches the input of the discriminator network.

Classifiers used

As already indicated above, the classifiers are used to provide better reliability during segmentation through accurate identification of the extracted sections from the satellite image. The classifiers not only help to improve the reliability of the extraction but also add a reinforcement mechanism that is accurate and contributes to the overall effectiveness of the system. This is effective primarily while dealing with a range of images that are required to be segmented accurately into seven identified classes.

A multi-layered perceptron (MLP) [106] which is a feed-forward Artificial Neural Network (ANN) with multiple hidden layers and trained with backpropagation (BP) algorithm, is used as a benchmark technique. Subsequently, Fuzzy C-Means (FCM) clustering technique using similarity measures like distance, connectivity, and intensity are used for generating decision clusters. Different similarity measures may be chosen based on the data or the application [99]. Thus, supervised (MLP) and unsupervised (FCM) approaches are taken during classification. Further, a few more classifiers namely soft-max, SVM, KNN, SOM, and PNN are used to test the effectiveness of the MLP and FCM classifiers for the content extraction from the satellite images. The softmax classifier is trained with the BP algorithm with stochastic gradient descent (SGD). For SVM, the radial basis function is selected as the kernel function. When KNN is used, the input is trained for seven classes and then the nearest neighbor algorithm is applied to split the individual color on the image. SOM is an unsupervised ANN that is used with 9×9 nodes and hexagonal topology. Again, PNN is also an unsupervised ANN which is trained with learning rate 0.04 and 1000 training step.

5.2.2   Learning Scheme of the semi-supervised adversarial network

The two networks discussed in Section 5.2.1 are trained with the semi-supervised adversarial algorithm (Fig. 5.1. The learning schemes of the networks are discussed in this section.

Let the input image be I_n of size $M \times N \times 3$. The segmentation network is denoted by $P(\cdot)$ and the output of the segmentation network is $P(I_n)$ of size $M \times N \times C$, where C denotes the total number of classes. The discriminator network is denoted by $Q(\cdot)$. Its input is the probability map of size $M \times N \times C$ either from the segmentation network or from the ground truth vector X_n. The output of the discriminator network is the confidence map of size $M \times N \times 1$.

The discriminator network is trained by minimizing the spatial cross-entropy loss with respect to the two classes (the prediction map from the segmentation network and the ground truth),

$$D_l = -\sum_{m,n}(1-x_n)\log(1-Q(P(I_n))^{(m,n)} + x_n\log(Q(X_n)^{(m,n)}) \qquad (5.1)$$

Here, if the input to the discriminator is the prediction maps of segmentation network ($P(I_n)$), then $x_n = 0$. Again, if the discriminator input is the ground truth (X_n) then $x_n = 1$. At pixel location (m,n), $Q(P(I_n))^{(m,n)}$ is the confidence map, when input to the discriminator is $P(I_n)$ and $Q(X_n)^{(m,n)}$ is the confidence map at location (m, n), when input to the discriminator is X_n.

The segmentation network is trained by minimizing the loss function,

$$S_{l_{total}} = L_c + \alpha_a L_a + \alpha_s L_s \qquad (5.2)$$

In Eqn. (5.2), α_a and α_s are the weights to minimize the loss.

$$L_C = -\sum_{m,n}\sum_{c \varepsilon C} X_{n_{(m,n,c)}} \log(P(I_n)_{(m,n,c)}) \qquad (5.3)$$

is called the spatial cross-entropy loss and,

$$L_a = -\sum_{m,n} \log(Q(P(I_n))^{(m,n)}) \qquad (5.4)$$

is the adversarial loss through which the adversarial learning process is carried out. Thus from Eqn. (5.2), when labeled image is used, the segmentation network is trained to minimize the loss,

$$S_{l_{labeled-image}} = L_c + \alpha_a L_a \qquad (5.5)$$

When the network is trained with unlabeled data, L_c is not used as there are no ground truth images. For an unlabeled image, I_n, at first the segmentation network produces a probability map $\widehat{X}$. This probability map $(\widehat{X})$ is used to train the discriminator network. The discriminator generates a confidence map $Q(P(\widehat{X}))$ which indicates that the prediction results' are nearly the same as that of the label maps of ground truth. By setting a threshold (γ_s) to the confidence map, the trustworthy regions in the prediction of the discriminator can be easily obtained. Thus the semi-supervised loss is given by,

$$L_s = -\sum_{m,n}\sum_{c \varepsilon C} U(Q(P(I_n))^{(m,n)} > \gamma_s).\widehat{X}_n^{(m,n,c)} \log(P(I_n)^{(m,n,c)}) \qquad (5.6)$$

Here, $\widehat{X}_n^{m,n,c} = 1$ when $C = argmaxP(I_n)^{(m,n,c)}$ and $U(\cdot)$ is the indicator function. As $\widehat{X}_n$ and the indicator function are taken as constants, Eqn. (5.6) can be called as masked spatial cross entropy loss. Thus from Eqn.(5.2), when unlabeled data is used, the segmentation network is trained to minimize the loss function,

$$S_{l_{unlabeled-image}} = \alpha_a L_a + \alpha_s L_s \qquad (5.7)$$

Thus, in the proposed work the discriminator network is trained to minimize the spatial cross-entropy loss with respect to two classes (ground truth and predictions from the segmentation network) given by Eqn. (5.1). Again, according to the semi-supervised adversarial algorithm, the segmentation network is trained with a multi-task loss function given by Eqn. (5.2). It means that when the segmentation network is trained with labeled images, it is tasked to minimize both the loss functions that are spatial cross-entropy loss with the ground truth labeled maps and the adversarial loss with the discriminator network. When the network is trained with unlabeled images, at first the initial prediction from the segmentation network is obtained. With this initial prediction from the segmentation network as input, the discriminator is trained and the confidence map is obtained. Then, based on a threshold value and with the confidence map, the semi-supervised loss is defined given by Eqn.(5.6). This loss is used as a supervisory signal to train the segmentation network in addition to the adversarial loss.

5.2.3   The Methodology

The block diagram of the proposed work is shown in Fig. 5.3. First, the inputs given to the system are high-resolution satellite images taken from the dataset of the DeepGlobe Land Cover Classification Challenge [108]. The dataset is the first public dataset of satellite images with high resolution which focuses mainly on rural areas. The total number of satellite images in the dataset is 1146 with 20448 × 20448 size. The dataset is divided into training, validation, and test images. The number of training images is 803 (70% of total images), validation is 171 (15% of total images) and test images are 171 (15% of total images). The images are

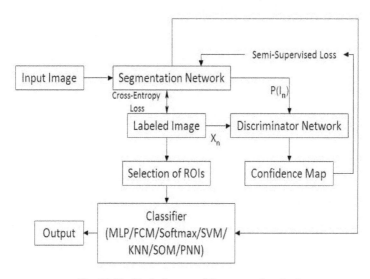

Fig. 5.3 The block diagram of the proposed method

RGB images, with 50 cm of pixel resolution and cover approximately 10716.9 km^2 of total area. Each image in the dataset is paired with label map annotation. The label image contains seven classes that follow the Anderson Classification [125]. The class distributions that are considered include the following: Forest Land (the land of trees where tree crown density is at least 20% with cuts that are clear), Agriculture Land (the place of cultivation done by human, examples can be: paddy fields, farmland of plantations, etc.), Rangeland (grassland, all other green lands except for forest and farm), Urban Land (the place of human-constructed structures), Barren Land (land with no plant life, hills, rocks, mountains, desert, seashore), Water (stream, waterway, reservoir, river, sea, ocean, lakes, ponds, pools, wetland) and Unknown region (others regions such as clouds).

Secondly, the segmentation network, which is a Deeplab-v2 framework with ResNet-101 [122], is trained for semantic segmentation whose outputs are the class probability maps with semantic categories given by $P(I_n)$. As the last layer of the network is a *softmax* layer, the probability of ith pixel x, in k^{th} batch, belonging to the cth class is given by,

$$p_c(x) = \frac{\exp(W_c^T f(\theta,x))}{\sum_{j=1}^{c} exp(W_j^T f(\theta,x))} \tag{5.8}$$

where, $W_c \varepsilon \Re^D$ weight matrix for the cth class of the last convolutional layer, D is the feature dimension, θ are the other parameters related to the last convolutional layer of the network and $f(\theta,x) \varepsilon \Re^D$ denotes the learned deep features of the network.

Thirdly, when the input to the discriminator is X_n, the output is $Q(X_n)$. Here, labeled images are considered and X_n is a ground truth image. For the unlabeled input case, the input to the discriminator network is $P(I_n)$ which is the predicted output obtained from the segmentation network. When the input is the ground truth image, the pixel values of the output of the discriminator network should be 1 and when the input is the images generated by the segmentation network then the pixel values of output the discriminator should be 0. This representation with correct class code enables the network to differentiate the ground truth and segmentation network predictions. But the segmentation network aims to generate images in such a way that the discriminator network cannot differentiate between the ground truth and the images generated by the segmentation network for better generation of the output by the segmentation network.

Fourthly, the loss functions used to train the discriminator network and the segmentation network are calculated as explained by Eqn.s (5.1) and (5.2) respectively. For the labeled images, the segmentation network is supervised by adversarial loss with the discriminator network and the cross-entropy loss with the ground truth label maps. For the unlabeled images, the segmentation network is trained with semi-supervised loss as a supervisory signal. With these losses as the supervisory signal, the segmentation network is trained to confuse the discriminator using the BP algorithm and the probability maps are obtained which are spatially close in similarity with the label maps of ground truth.

Next, to train the supervised classifiers, the target to the classifiers is fixed by selecting the RoIs from the ground truth labeled images. The RoIs are selected by setting the pixel values of RoIs as 1 and others as 0.

Subsequently, the output of the segmentation network $P(I_n)$ is then fed to the classifiers to obtain the RoIs in the satellite images. As already discussed, a total of seven classifiers are used for this purpose and the results of each of the classifiers are compared. The first classifier is the MLP with two hidden layers and trained using the BP algorithm. It is used to extract different regions as outlined above. The target of the classifier is the values of the pixel of different regions in the image. A particular region is selected as a target by setting the pixel values of RoIs as 1 and others as 0. When the FCM classifier is used, the image is first converted to $L \times a \times b$ color space as it enables to quantify the visual differences in colors of the images. Then the FCM algorithm is applied to the satellite image, to cluster different regions. Here, the grouping of pixel values is done by reducing the Euclidean distances to a minimum between pixels and the corresponding cluster center. The algorithm outputs the index values to the clusters. Then every pixel of the image is labeled with these index values. Thus the pixel values of particular regions in the images are the outputs of the classifier. The other classifiers used are Softmax classifier, SVM, KNN, SOM, and PNN.

Finally, the outputs of the classifiers obtained are the required RoIs of satellite images. The experiments are initiated with direct input feeding and then are repeated with other feeding methods. It makes the training robust.

5.3 Results and Discussion

The experimental results are discussed in the following sections. In Section 5.3.1, the results obtained for the semi-supervised adversarial network are discussed. The results obtained from the classifiers are discussed in Section 5.3.2.

5.3.1   Results obtained from semi-supervised adversarial network

In the proposed method, the segmentation network is trained using the SGD optimization method. In this method, weight decay is set to 10^{-5} and the momentum is taken to be 0.9. Also, 2.5×10^{-5} initial learning rate is considered, and the power of 0.9 polynomial decay is used to decrease the learning rate [120]. Adam optimizer [126] with the learning rate 10^{-4} is used for the discriminator training and the polynomial decay with the power of 0.9 is used. In this method, α_a is set as 0.01, and α_s and γ_s are taken to be 0.2.

Cropping and random scaling methods are utilized to make the image dimension of 321×321 in the training process. Here, to train the network, 5000 iterations are used and batch size is set to 10.

As the semi-supervised algorithm requires both labeled and unlabeled data, to validate the semi-supervised algorithm, 12.5% and 50% ($\frac{1}{8}th$ and $\frac{1}{2}th$) portion of the total data are sampled as labeled inputs to the system. The rest of the training images are used as unlabeled data. The amount of data 12.5% and 50% ($\frac{1}{8}th$ and $\frac{1}{2}th$) of the data are chosen randomly for the experimental purpose. The method is compared with existing methods, VGG-16 [114], ResNet [55], RCNN [116], [120], Deeplab-v2 [122] and SegNet [8]. Table 5.1 shows the comparison of the proposed method when the two networks are trained with input images with only labeled data (proposed method with labeled data) and both labeled and unlabeled data (proposed method with the semi-supervised algorithm) with different existing methods. Here, the inputs are fed to the network using direct feeding. In the proposed method with labeled data, experiments are performed with the full amount of data as labeled inputs as well as both 12.5% and 50% ($\frac{1}{8}th$ and $\frac{1}{2}th$) portions of data as labeled input. When experiments are performed with 12.5% and 50% ($\frac{1}{8}th$ and $\frac{1}{2}th$) portions of data as labeled input, the rest training images are taken unlabeled. Similarly in the proposed method with the semi-supervised algorithm, the experiments are performed with both 12.5% and 50% ($\frac{1}{8}th$ and $\frac{1}{2}th$) portions of data as labeled input, and rest images are taken as unlabeled.

In Table 5.1, results are shown when trained with 12.5% ($\frac{1}{8}th$) amount of data obtained using the proposed method. The mean IOU of the proposed method with labeled data is 67.26 and the mean IOU of the proposed method with the semi-supervised algorithm is 68.26. Again when trained with 50% ($\frac{1}{2}th$) amount of data, the proposed method generates a mean IOU of 67.64 with labeled data and for the semi-supervised algorithm, it is 68.46. It is seen that the mean IOU of the proposed method is increased by 2.24% compared to that of [120] and 10.2% than that of VGG-16 [114].

The SSIM of the proposed method with labeled data is 0.8254 and the SSIM of the proposed method with the semi-supervised algorithm is 0.8453. Again, when trained with 50% ($\frac{1}{2}th$) amount of data, the proposed method generates an SSIM of 0.8375 with labeled data and for the semi-supervised algorithm, it is 0.8523. It is seen that the SSIM of the proposed method is increased by 4.9% than that in [120] and 15.6% than that of VGG-16 [114].

Again, the pixel accuracy metric for the proposed method with labeled data is 87.13 and the pixel accuracy metric of the proposed method with the semi-supervised algorithm is 87.68. Further, when trained with 50% ($\frac{1}{2}th$) amount of data, the proposed method generates a pixel accuracy of 87.35 with labeled data and for the semi-supervised algorithm, it is 87.96. It is seen that the pixel accuracy of the proposed method is increased by 2.5% compared to that in [120] and 7.4% than that of VGG-16 [114]. Thus, the proposed method with the semi-supervised algorithm (unlabeled data) gives better results than the other state-of-the-art methods.

In Table 5.2, the analysis of different values of α_s and γ_s with 50% (1/2) amount of data and with the semi-supervised algorithm are shown. At first, the values of α_a is set to 0.1 and γ_s to 0 for comparison. At this point, the proposed method achieves a mean IOU of 41.71% when α_s is set to 0.1. Again, both the values of α_a and γ_s are set to 0.1. Then the highest mean IOU of 68.12% is achieved for $\alpha_s = 0.2$. After that, the results are obtained

Table 5.1 Comparison of the proposed method with different existing methods

| Methods | mean IOU | | | SSIM | | | Pixel Accuracy | | |
| | Amount of data | | | Amount of data | | | Amount of data | | |
	1/8	1/2	Full	1/8	1/2	Full	1/8	1/2	Full
VGG-16 [114]	Not Applicable	Not Applicable	62.13	Not Applicable	Not Applicable	0.7367	Not Applicable	Not Applicable	81.87
RCNN [116]	Not Applicable	Not Applicable	62.87	Not Applicable	Not Applicable	0.7424	Not Applicable	Not Applicable	82.19
ResNet [55]	Not Applicable	Not Applicable	63.46	Not Applicable	Not Applicable	0.7487	Not Applicable	Not Applicable	82.79
SegNet [8]	Not Applicable	Not Applicable	64.42	Not Applicable	Not Applicable	0.7504	Not Applicable	Not Applicable	83.29
DeepLab-v2 [122]	Not Applicable	Not Applicable	66.67	Not Applicable	Not Applicable	0.7684	Not Applicable	Not Applicable	84.56
Method in [120] with labeled data	66.71	66.86	66.96	0.7854	0.7936	0.7972	85.46	85.68	85.81
Method in [120] with Semi-supervised algo-rithm	67.12	67.23	Not Applicable	0.8034	0.8120	Not Applicable	86.24	86.78	Not Applicable
Proposed Method with labeled data	67.26	67.64	67.76	0.8254	0.8375	0.8395	87.13	87.35	87.46
Proposed Method with Semi-supervised algo-rithm	68.26	68.46	Not Applicable	0.8453	0.8523	Not Applicable	87.68	87.96	Not Applicable

Table 5.2 Analysis of different values of α_s and γ_s with 50% (1/2) amount of data

Data Amount	α_a	α_s	γ_s	Mean IoU
1/2	0.1	0	0	41.62
1/2	0.1	0.05	0	41.69
1/2	0.1	0.1	0	41.71
1/2	0.1	0.05	0.1	67.46
1/2	0.1	0.1	0.1	67.84
1/2	0.1	0.2	0.1	68.12
1/2	0.1	0.3	0.1	67.93
1/2	0.1	0.2	0.2	68.46
1/2	0.1	0.2	0.3	67.41

with different values of γ_s by setting α_a and α_s to 0.1 and 0.2 respectively. The γ_s is increased gradually. The method performs with satisfactory results for the values of γ_s in a range from 0.1 to 0.3, but the highest mean IOU can be achieved when γ_s is 0.2. Similarly, as shown in Table 5.3, the analysis of different values of α_s and γ_s with 12.5% (1/8) amount of data and with the semi-supervised algorithm indicate the advantages of the proposed method. Here also at first, the values of α_a are set to 0.1 and γ_s to 0 for comparison. At that point, the proposed method achieved a mean IOU of 48.92% when α_s is set to 0.1. Again, both the values of α_a and γ_s are set to 0.1. Then the highest mean IOU of 68.02% is achieved for $\alpha_s = 0.2$. After that, the results are obtained with different values of γ_s by setting α_a and α_s to 0.1 and 0.2 respectively. The value of γ_s is increased gradually. Here also, the method performs with satisfactory results for the values of γ_s in a range from 0.1 to 0.3, but the highest mean IOU can be achieved when γ_s is 0.2. When $\gamma_s = 0$, all the input images become unlabeled (as per Eqn. (5.6)). As a result, the performance of the network suffers because pixels predictions are taking place with unlabeled images. It means that the semi-supervised approach (with unlabeled images and supervised training) is better suited for the purpose.

From Table 5.1 it is seen that the proposed method, when trained with the semi-supervised algorithm (when both labeled and unlabeled data are used) gives better results when compared with other existing methods. Subsequently, in Table 5.4 a comparison of the proposed method

Table 5.3 Analysis of different values of α_s and γ_s with 12.5% (1/8) amount of data

Data Amount	α_a	α_s	γ_s	Mean IoU
1/8	0.1	0	0	48.23
1/8	0.1	0.05	0	48.67
1/8	0.1	0.1	0	48.92
1/8	0.1	0.05	0.1	67.36
1/8	0.1	0.1	0.1	67.78
1/8	0.1	0.2	0.1	68.02
1/8	0.1	0.3	0.1	67.88
1/8	0.1	0.2	0.2	68.26
1/8	0.1	0.2	0.3	67.57

Table 5.4 Comparison of the proposed method with different input feeding mechanism

Input feeding	mean IOU Amount of data		SSIM Amount of data		Pixel Accuracy Amount of data	
	1/8	1/2	1/8	1/2	1/8	1/2
Direct feeding of input	68.26	68.46	0.8453	0.8523	87.68	87.96
Feeding of input with time delay	68.76	68.92	0.8544	0.8615	88.52	88.90
Feeding of input with filters	69.51	69.67	0.8586	0.8666	88.96	89.34
Scrambled input feed	70.41	70.58	0.8716	0.8796	90.37	90.77

with the semi-supervised algorithm with different input feeding mechanism are shown. It is seen that when trained with 50% ($\frac{1}{2}$) amount of data, the scrambled input feed method gives better results than the other feeding methods. After a series of experiments with stride and learning rate valuations, it is seen that the mean IOU when trained with the scrambled input feed method, has increased by 3.1% than the direct feeding of input approach, 2.4% than the feeding of input images with time delay for sample augmentation method and 1.3% than the feeding of input images with noise removal, edge sharpening for sample augmentation method. Again, the SSIM when trained with the scrambled input feed method has increased by 3.2% than the direct feeding of input method, 2.1% than the feeding of input images with time delay for sample augmentation method and 1.5% than the feeding of input images with noise removal, edge sharpening for sample augmentation method. Similarly, the pixel accuracy value when trained with the scrambled input feed method has increased by 3.2% than the direct feeding of input method, 2.1% than the feeding of input images for sample augmentation with time delay method and 1.6% than the feeding of input images with noise removal, edge sharpening for sample augmentation method. These results are obtained from average readings of several rounds of tedious training and testing with variations in the learning rate, stride, and filter masks. Though the results obtained in Table 4 are not spectacularly significant, these methods play an important role in the work as these are derived using limited numbers of training samples. It means the proposed approach is useful when there is an insufficient number of samples with annotations for training. Also, the seemingly less significant improvements have validated the role played by context feed, bootstrapping, diversity in data, and correlation in expanding the learning profile of a semi-adversarial network configured for satellite image segment extraction. It also has contributed in improving the accuracy and reliability of the network.

Fig.s 5.4 and 5.5 show the performance curve of the model i.e. the segmentation and the discriminator network losses with iteration. In this method, the discriminator network is

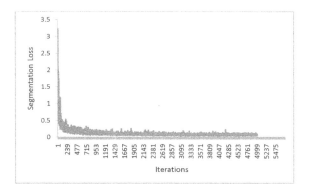

Fig. 5.4 Iteration Vs Segmentation loss

used to differentiate the input given to it. The input to the discriminator network is either the ground truth image or the predicted images which are generated by the segmentation network. In Fig.s 5.4 and 5.5, it can be seen that the segmentation network loss and the discriminator loss when dealing with ground truth images are converging to some finite values. The segmentation loss is in the range of 0.1 to 0.2 and the discriminator loss when dealing with ground truth images is in the range of 0.2 to 0.3. Again, in Fig. 5.5, the loss curve of the discriminator network when dealing with the predicted image generated by the segmentation network is increasing. In this case, the discriminator network is giving output as 1 (it should give output as 0 as it is the input image generated by the segmentation network but could not differentiate the input) and for this reason, the loss is increasing showing the goal of the segmentation network is achieved. It signifies that the model (the semi-supervised algorithm to train the segmentation and discriminator network) has reached some optimum state, and it cannot improve any further. It implies the learning is sufficient. The convergence plots show fluctuations as learning time performance varies.

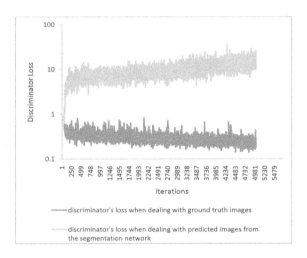

Fig. 5.5 Iterations Vs Discriminator loss when dealing with ground truth images and predicted images from the segmentation network

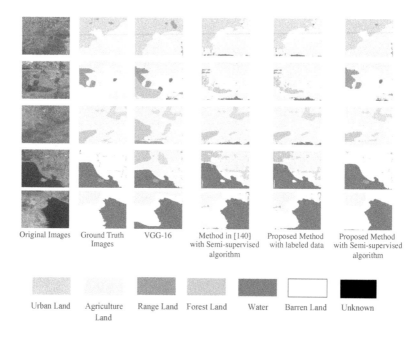

Original Images   Ground Truth   VGG-16   Method in [140]   Proposed Method   Proposed Method
                  Images   with Semi-supervised with labeled data   with Semi-supervised
                                            algorithm   algorithm

Urban Land   Agriculture   Range Land   Forest Land   Water   Barren Land   Unknown
              Land

Fig. 5.6 Comparisons with 50% (1/2) amount of data

Fig. 5.6 shows output images when trained with 50% (1/2) amounts of data as labeled data and rest as unlabeled. The network is trained for 7 different classes as mentioned earlier. Here the input feeding method considered is the scrambled input feed. In the figure, the proposed work is compared with the work [120] and VGG-16 [114].

5.3.2   Experimental results for the classifier

From Tables 5.1 and 5.4, it is seen that when trained with the semi-supervised algorithm (with both labeled and unlabeled data) and with the scrambled input feed method, the segmentation network gives better performance. Now, with these outputs of the segmentation network as input, an MLP is trained to segment the satellite images with various RoIs. The pixel values of various RoIs are taken as the target of the system. The MLP is trained with the BP algorithm for around 1000 iterations (extended over to a number of cycles) and 10^{-4} as the learning rate. At first, different training functions such as Levenberg-Marquardt (LM), Scaled conjugate gradient (SCG), Conjugate gradient back-propagation with Polak-ribiere updates, Bayesian Regulation back-propagation (BRBP), Resilient back-propagation (RBP), etc. are used to train the classifier. Then, between the classifier output and target image, the MSE is calculated for all the training types. Among all the training types, the LM back-propagation shows better MSE convergence. The network is then trained with the different number of hidden layers i.e. single, double, and triple. The numbers of neurons in hidden layers are altered and LM back-propagation training is used to train the classifier for around 1000 iterations (extended over to a number of cycles) and 10^{-5} learning rate. After that, for the images, MSE and SSIM between the classifier output and target image are calculated. The experimental results obtained show that double hidden layered MLP gives better results in terms of MSE [105][106]. The architecture of MLP with the double hidden layer is shown in Fig. 5.7.

The FCM classifier is also used to discriminate regions in the satellite images. Similarly, other classifiers such as softmax, SVM, KNN, SOM, and PNN are also used with parameters discussed earlier. Then MSE and SSIM between the classifier output and the RoIs are calculated. Table 5.5 shows the comparison of MSE and SSIM values for different regions of the output of all the classifiers. Among the classifiers, the softmax classifier gives better results in terms of MSE and SSIM but the computational time is higher than the other classifiers. This may be optimized with better hardware and modularity in the programming approach. In the case of MSE, softmax is 6.7% better than MLP and 5.2% better than FCM. Similarly, in the case of SSIM, softmax is 1% better than MLP and 1.4% better than FCM. In Table 5.6, the summary of the performance of the classifiers used to extract RoIs of satellite images is shown in terms of True Positive (TP), True Negative (TN), False Positive (FP)

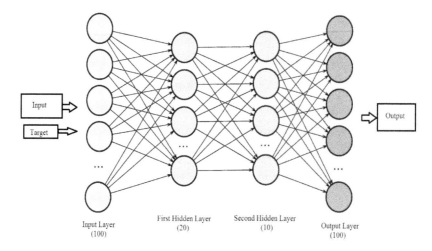

Fig. 5.7 Architecture of the MLP with double hidden layer

and False Negative (FN). Fig. 5.8 shows the comparison of the output of MLP, FCM, and softmax classifier.

The experiments carried out and the results obtained indicate that the semi-supervised adversarial learning method used to extract different RoIs of satellite images is effective despite having limited availability of appropriate prior information. The algorithm being semi-supervised has used both labeled and unlabelled data for generating better results. The method has been tested with four different input feeding mechanisms such as direct feeding of input, feeding of input images with time delay for sample augmentation, feeding of input images with noise removal, edge sharpening, and scrambled input feed which enhances the quality of input data by contributing higher correlation. Also, the results obtained from the classifiers are compared. It is observed that the softmax classifier gives better results than other classifiers. Thus, the advantage of the proposed approach is obvious.

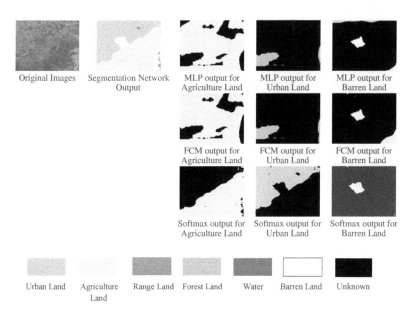

Fig. 5.8 Comparison of the output of the MLP, FCM and softmax classifier.

Table 5.5 Comparison of MSE and SSIM values for different regions of the output of the classifier

Regions	MLP			FCM			Softmax		
	Time required in seconds	MSE	SSIM	Time required in seconds	MSE	SSIM	Time required in seconds	MSE	SSIM
Urban land	44.65	0.0064	0.8982	14.65	0.0967	0.8896	46.26	0.0053	0.9023
Agricultural land	30.25	0.0160	0.8946	10.25	0.0260	0.8886	31.41	0.0120	0.9012
Range land	41.71	0.0066	0.8986	21.71	0.0354	0.8892	42.43	0.0054	0.9064
Forest land	64.33	0.0765	0.8944	34.33	0.0768	0.8884	65.42	0.0623	0.9054
Water	55.93	0.0062	0.8985	35.93	0.0874	0.8883	56.10	0.0051	0.9043
Barren land	145.04	0.0348	0.8984	65.04	0.0446	0.8891	146.13	0.0292	0.9026
Unknown region	80.31	0.0281	0.8981	40.31	0.0549	0.8894	81.23	0.0262	0.9023

Regions	SVM			KNN			SOM		
	Time required in seconds	MSE	SSIM	Time required in seconds	MSE	SSIM	Time required in seconds	MSE	SSIM
Urban land	32.15	0.0977	0.8865	48.12	0.0988	0.8712	11.76	0.0986	0.8782
Agricultural land	26.30	0.0466	0.8846	36.46	0.0568	0.8720	10.10	0.0563	0.8763
Range land	37.14	0.0592	0.8854	42.63	0.0686	0.8713	18.54	0.0623	0.8742
Forest land	44.23	0.0828	0.8863	69.43	0.0856	0.8729	29.56	0.0836	0.8765
Water	46.13	0.0889	0.8843	59.41	0.0902	0.8734	30.45	0.0892	0.8772
Barren land	144.23	0.0513	0.8846	148.26	0.0582	0.8726	130.12	0.0543	8785
Unknown region	70.65	0.0602	0.8863	84.63	0.0676	0.8732	35.62	0.0639	0.8769

Regions	PNN		
	Time required in seconds	MSE	SSIM
Urban land	10.12	0.0826	0.8974
Agricultural land	09.92	0.0146	0.8972
Range land	15.16	0.0245	0.8973
Forest land	27.65	0.0628	0.8969
Water	24.12	0.0748	0.8968
Barren land	128.65	0.0326	0.8975
Unknown region	30.12	0.0427	0.8978

Table 5.6 Summary of classifier performance while extracting RoI of satellite images (shown in terms of True Positive (TP), True Negative (TN), False Positive (FP) and False Negative (FN))

Type	Average process time in Sec.	TP in %	TN in %	FP in %	FN in %
MLP	145.04	89.6	6.2	3.2	1.0
FCM	140.62	86.8	4.2	6.4	2.6
Softmax	146.13	92.4	5.6	1.6	0.4
SVM	144.23	85.3	6.7	5.3	2.7
KNN	148.26	80.3	8.9	6.8	4.0
SOM	130.12	82.6	7.8	5.3	4.3
PNN	128.65	87.2	5.3	4.0	3.5

5.3.3   Comparative study and discussion

Table 5.8 shows the comparison of the proposed methods explained in Chapter 3, Chapter 4, and Chapter 5 with two existing methods described in [15] and [104]. Since double hidden layer with hidden neuron number [20 10] and LMBP Training function gives better results, therefore, the results obtained with these combinations are shown here. From the table 5.8 it was seen that the proposed method described in Chapter 5 gives better results both in terms of MSE and Accuracy. For the 'Grass' region the performances of the methods discussed in Section 3.2 and 3.3 and Section 4.2 and that reported in [15] and [104] are best. The best performance of the proposed method Chapter 2 is considered for comparison The combination of two hidden layer MLP (20,10) and the semi-supervised method with softmax produces MSE of 0.0014 which is 14.2% better than the value obtained with the method discussed in Chapter 4. This is 12.5 times better than that reported in [15] and 11.7 times superior to the results presented in [104]. The corresponding improvement in accuracy is 5.8% and 4.8%. This indicates the advantage of the proposed approach.

Table 5.7 Parameters used in the proposed method

Segmentation Network	
Training iteration	5000
Learning Rate	2.5×10^{-5}
optimizer	SGD
batch size	10
Weight decay	10^{-5}
crop size	321×321
Discriminator Network	
Training iteration	5000
Learning Rate	10^{-4}
optimizer	Adam
batch size	10
Weight decay	10^{-5}
crop size	321×321
MLP	
Training iteration	1000
Learning Rate	10^{-4}
training function	LM Back propagation
Number of hidden layer	2
number of hidden neuron	20 and 10
FCM	
Number of cluster	7
Fuzzy weight value	2

Table 5.8 Comparison of the proposed method with existing methods

Sl. No.	Methods	MSE	Accuracy in %
1.	MLP + manual labeling	0.0019	92.17
2.	MLP+KMC	0.0018	92.67
3.	SegNet+KMC+MLP	0.0016	93.28
4.	SegNet+KMC+softmax	0.0015	93.46
5.	GAN+MLP	0.0015	95.65
6.	GAN+softmax	0.0014	95.83
7	S. Arumuga Devi et.al.[15]	0.0189	90.21
8	A. Hassanat et.al [104]	0.0178	91.23

5.4   Conclusion

For automated and continuous extraction of content from satellite images using learning-based approaches, efficient training of a deep learning network requires adequate prior knowledge which may not be available in all cases. Here, the semi-supervised adversarial learning method has been presented to extract different RoIs of satellite images. The method deals with the extraction of meaningful content from satellite images using learning-based approaches with the limited availability of appropriate prior information. To validate the proposed method, the DeepGlobe Land Cover Classification Challenge dataset is used. In the proposed method, in addition to unlabeled data, some supervision is also adopted to train a composite network. It consists of two learning-based networks used for segmentation and discrimination which are trained with the adversarial algorithm. The algorithm being semi-supervised uses both labeled and unlabeled data for generating better results. Finally, the outputs of the segmentation network are used as input to train a classifier to extract the RoIs of the satellite images. The classifiers used are MLP (supervised), softmax (supervised), SVM (supervised), KNN (supervised), SOM (unsupervised), PNN (unsupervised), and FCM (unsupervised). The method is tested with four different input feeding mechanisms such as direct feeding of input, feeding of input images with time delay for sample augmentation, feeding of input images with noise removal, edge sharpening, and scrambled input feed which enhances the quality of input data by contributing higher correlation. The results of the adversarial network are compared with some of the state-of-the-art works. The results obtained from the classifiers are also compared. It is observed that the softmax classifier gives better results than other classifiers. Though the semi-supervised adversarial method is reliable to overcome the problem of limited training data of high-resolution satellite images, these images have another serious problem. The images are often contaminated by random noise during the acquisition and transmission phase which may impact the overall segmentation results. Therefore, to overcome the problem of noise which is inherently present during acquisition, an contractive autoencoder based method is discussed in the next chapter.

6

Segmentation of Satellite Images using Contractive Autoencoder (CAE) Aided Deep Learning Approach

In Chapter 5, the method based on semi-supervised adversarial learning with different input feeding mechanisms and a learning-based classifier proved to be reliable for segmentation of different regions from satellite images where training and annotated data are limited. But in some specific situations, the input images may contain noise during acquisition which may affect the performance of the segmentation process. For such a situation, a contractive autoencoder aided deep learning-based approach is reported in this chapter.[5]

6.1 Introduction

A good understanding and insights of the retrieved information from the images obtained from a satellite are necessary for many real-life applications such as weather prediction, flood prediction, deforestation, etc. [134]. To analyze a satellite image properly, the extraction of the different regions in the image is a crucial and important task. The automating of extraction of the different regions of these data has been addressed by the researchers in different ways over the years. In the last few years, ML and DL-based techniques have proven to be successful and strong prospects for this purpose. The state of the art, DL-aided approaches have been adopted for satellite image analysis during the last decade [113]. The semantic segmentation using the DeepLab v3+ [135] model and VGG-16 [114] of farm areas in low-resolution satellite images was presented in [136]. Again, in [137] the encoder-decoder architecture for SegNet [8] based network was used to identify buildings, vegetation, and buildings on high-resolution satellite images. The authors in [64] had developed a method for automatic extraction of information from a large size date set of satellite images. They had used SegNet [8] and U- Net [48] for this purpose. An approach for water surface segmentation from satellite images was presented in [138]. The method was based on the application of a U-Net [48] and a transfer knowledge-based model. In [139] the author used AffinityNet [140] to perform direct semantic segmentation in images. Similarly in [141] the

---

[5]A part of this work is reported in

1. M. Barthakur and K.K. Sarma, "Segmentation of Satellite Images using Contractive Autoencoder (CAE) Aided Deep Learning Approach", in proceedings of Springer 3rd Virtual International Conference on Intelligent Computing and Advances in Communication, (ICAC-2020), Bhubaneswar, Odisha, Nov.,2020. **(The paper is selected as the best paper in the session Intelligent Computing-I)**

U- net [48] architecture was used to perform semantic segmentation of clouds in satellite images by utilizing the transfer learning method. In this thesis also we have presented both ML and DL-based methods in the previous chapters where the results show the methods are reliable for real-life applications.

Though the above-mentioned methods are beneficial for extraction of different regions from high-resolution satellite images, the images are often contaminated by random noise during the acquisition and transmission phase. The overall noise characteristics depend on many factors, such as sensor type, temperature, illumination, exposure time and interference during transmission [145], [146], [147]. The existence of noise not only degrades the visual quality but also restricts the subsequent processing by leading to erroneous results. Linear and non-linear spatial domain filters such as lowpass, band-pass, median and min/max filters, frequency-domain methods, wavelet methods are frequently used methods for removal of noise in literature [98]. While many techniques exist for noise removal and they have achieved reasonably good performance in image denoising, the methods suffered from several drawbacks [148], including the need for optimization methods for the test phase, manual setting parameters, and a certain model for single denoising tasks. Recently, as architectures became more flexible, deep learning techniques gained the ability to overcome these drawbacks [148].

In this work, a deep learning-based method to extract different regions of interest(RoIs)is presented in which a DL-based noise removal process from the input high-resolution satellite images is also included. In the work, at first, the high-resolution satellite images are processed with the Contractive Autoencoder (CAE) to remove the noise which is inherently present in the images during acquisition. The output of the CAE is taken as input to train a segmentation network which is a deep neural network. Finally, the output of the segmentation network is used to train both supervised and unsupervised classifiers to extract different RoIs from the satellite images. Here, the DeepGlobe Land Cover Classification Challenge [108] dataset is

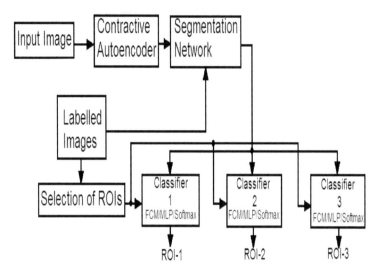

Fig. 6.1 The block diagram of the proposed method

used to validate the results obtained. Experimental results show the method is reliable for real-time applications.

6.2   The Proposed method

In this section, the proposed method is discussed briefly. At first, the architecture of the proposed system and finally the methodology is discussed.

6.2.1   Architecture of the network

In the proposed approach, the CAE is used for de-noising the satellite images. For semantic segmentation, a segmentation network is designed and finally, three classifiers are used to extract the required RoIs from the satellite images. A detailed description of all these networks is presented here.

Contractive Autoencoder:

The Contractive Autoencoder (CAE) [142] is used to reduce the noise present in the satellite images during acquisition. It also makes the output less varying due to the variation in the input. Here, the input, I, is encoded by the CAE using function g, and to make the output identical to the input, the encoded values $g(I)$ are decoded with a function h. As the objective of the CAE is to obtain a vigorous representation of the learned pattern, therefore, to make the output less sensitive to the small variations in the input, a penalty term called the Frobenius norm of the Jacobian matrix (J_f) added to the loss function of the CAE. J_f is the sum of the square of all the elements and it is calculated with respect to the inputs for the hidden layers. Therefore, the loss function of the CAE is given by,

$$l = |I - h(g(I)| + \lambda \|J_F(I)\|_F^2 \tag{6.1}$$

$$\|J_F(I)\|_F^2 = \sum_{i,j} (\frac{\partial h_j(I)}{\partial I_i})^2 \tag{6.2}$$

where, λ is the coefficient of weight decay which controls the relative importance of regularization.

Segmentation Network:

For the semantic segmentation of the satellite images, the Deeplab-v2 [122] framework with ResNet-101 [115] model is used as the segmentation network. To match the output of the network with the input image size the strides of the last two layers of the ResNet-101 [115] model are taken as 1. In the conv4 and conv5 layers of the network, to make the receptive field enlarge, dilated convolution [144] is applied with 2 and 4 strides respectively. Again as the architecture of ResNet-101 [115] does not have an upsampling layer before the final classification layer, therefore to match the size of the output of the segmentation network with the input image and to make the resolution better, the last classification layer of the

ResNet-101 is removed and an upsampling layer with the softmax layer is applied as the final layer of the network. These variations also make the proposed method robust [143].

Classifier used:

The classifiers used in this work, provide better reliability in the segmentation process by accurately identifying the regions of the satellite images to be extracted. In this work, both supervised and unsupervised classifiers are used to check the robustness of the work. As an unsupervised classifier, the Fuzzy C-Means (FCM) [99] is used. Based on the application and data, different similarity measures such as intensity, connectivity, and distance are used in the clustering process to generate a decision cluster. Again, as the supervised classifier, multi-layer perceptron (MPL) [106] and softmax classifier [143] is used in this work. Both the MLP and softmax classifiers are trained with the backpropagation algorithm. The classifiers also add an accurate and strengthening mechanism to contribute to the effectiveness of the work. While dealing with a large set of images to be accurately segmented, these classifiers are effective and reliable in the proposed work.

6.2.2 Methodology

In the work, the input to the system is the dataset of high-resolution satellite images. The dataset is obtained from DeepGlobe Land Cover Classification Challenge [108]. The dataset consists of a total of 1146 images of size 20448×20448 which are high-resolution satellite images of rural areas. The label map annotation image for each of the satellite images is also there in the dataset. The images are divided with 803 (70% of total images) number of training images, 171 (15% of total images) number of images for validation, and 171 (15% of total images) number of test images. In the images, Forest Land, Agriculture Land, Rangeland, Urban Land, Barren Land, Water, and Unknown region are the class distribution considered for segmentation in the proposed system.

At first, as shown in the block diagram in Fig. 6.1, the input images are fed to the CAE. The CAE consists of one input layer, one hidden layer, and one output layer. The loss function used to train the CAE is given by equation 6.1. The output images of the CAE are the de-noised reconstructed images.

Next, the de-noised images obtained from the CAE, are taken as the input to the segmentation network. Here, the network is a a Deeplab-v2 [122] framework with ResNet-101 [115]. The network is trained to obtain the semantic segmentation of the satellite images. The output images of the network are the maps of class probabilities with semantic categories. As explained earlier, the last layer of the segmentation network is the softmax layer, and therefore, the probability of the xth pixel i which belongs to the kth class and in c^{th} batch is given by,

$$p_k(i) = \frac{\exp(w_k^T l(\alpha, i))}{\sum_{j=1}^{k} exp(w_j^T l(\alpha, i))} \qquad (6.3)$$

where F denotes the feature dimension, w^k weight matrix for the kth class of the last convolutional layer, $l(\alpha, i)$ is the learned deep features of the network, and α are the other parameters related to the last convolutional layer of the segmentation network [143].

Thirdly, to train the MLP and the softmax classifier, the targets are fixed by selecting the particular RoIs from the labeled maps of ground truth images. The selection is done by keeping the pixel values of the RoIs as 1 and other pixel values as 0.

Subsequently, the semantic maps obtained from the segmentation network are taken as input to the classifiers. To extract a specific RoI from the output of the segmentation network, one classifier is used. That means when the unsupervised classifier is used, for the seven RoIs, seven FCM classifiers are used. Similarly when supervised classifiers are used, at first seven MLP classifiers are trained to obtain for the three RoIs and then three softmax classifiers are trained for each of the RoIs. In the block diagram in Fig. 6.1 only three classifiers are shown for three RoIs for better understanding. For the FCM classifier, the output of the segmentation network is at first converted $L \times a \times b$ color space. This is done as the $L \times a \times b$ color space quantifies the visual difference of the colors in the images. Then, to cluster the required RoIs, the FCM algorithm is applied to the images. In the algorithm, the grouping of the pixel values of the RoIs in the images is done by minimizing the Euclidean distance between the cluster center and the pixel. The outputs of the algorithm are the index values to the clusters and therefore, with these values every pixel is labeled in the image. Thus the FCM classifier outputs the required RoIs. Again, when an MLP classifier is used, it is trained with two hidden layers. The training is done with the BP algorithm. When the softmax classifier is used it is trained with the BP algorithm and with stochastic gradient descent (SGD). The different classifiers are used to check which classifier is suitable for the proposed system and makes the system robust. Finally, the outputs obtained from the classifiers are the required RoIs of the satellite images.

6.3   Results and Discussion

In the proposed method, the CAE is trained with one hidden layer and the number of the hidden neuron is taken as 75. as discussed earlier the loss is calculated with Equ. 6.1 and here the value of the weight regularization parameter is taken as 0.005. The CAE is trained for a maximum of 5000 iterations. The peak signal to noise ratio (PSNR) value between the input satellite image and the output reconstructed image is calculated after an interval of 1000 iteration. In Fig. 6.2, a graph between the PSNR value and the iteration is shown. The output of the CAE obtained after 5000 iterations is taken as the input to the segmentation network.

At first, the segmentation network is trained with the input as the original satellite image. Then the value of mean Intersection Over Union (IOU), Structural Similarity Index (SSIM), and Pixel Accuracy is calculated. Then the network is trained with the input as the output of CAE. Then again the values mean IOU, SSIM, and pixel accuracy are calculated. The

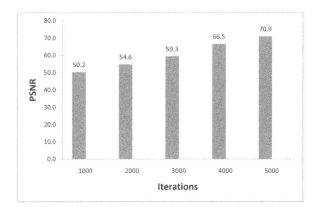

Fig. 6.2 Iteration Vs PSNR values for CAE

Table 6.1 Comparison of the results obtained for output of the Segmentation Network with input as original image and output of CAE

Input to the segmentation network	mean IOU	SSIM	Pixel Accuracy
Original Image	80.35	0.8458	81.73
Output of CAE	88.42	0.9035	89.78

comparison of these values is shown in Table 6.1. It is seen that when the segmentation network is trained with the output of the CAE, the mean IOU is 10.04%, SSIM is 6.8% and pixel accuracy is 9.8% better than the output of the network when trained with original images. The network is trained with the SGD optimization method and the weight decay is set to 10^{-5}. The momentum is taken to be 0.9 and initial learning rate is set as 2.5×10^{-5} [143]. In Fig. 6.3 the comparison of the output of the segmentation network with input as the original images and the output of CAE is shown.

With the output of the segmentation network, the classifiers are trained. at first, the FCM classifier is used to obtained different RoIs from the output of the segmentation network. Then the supervised classifiers, the MLP, and the softmax classifier are trained to obtain the required RoIs. The MLP is trained with a double hidden layer where the number of hidden

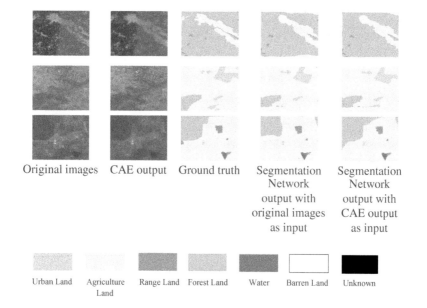

Fig. 6.3 Comparison of the output of the Segmentation Network with input as original image and output of CAE

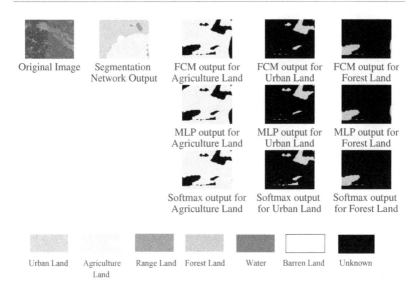

Fig. 6.4 Comparison of the output of the FCM, MLP and softmax classifier.

neurons for the first and second hidden layer is taken as 25 and 50 respectively. It is trained with Levenberg-Marquardt (LM) training function. The softmax classifier is trained with the SGD method as discussed earlier. Both the MLP and the softmax classifier are trained for 1000 iterations. In Table 6.2, the comparison of mean square error (MSE) and SSIM values for different regions of the output of all the classifiers are shown. From the table, it is seen that the softmax classifier gives better results than the other classifiers. It is seen that the MSE, SSIM, and pixel accuracy of softmax is 6.7%, 5.4%, and 3.2% respectively, better than the MLP and 8.4%, 6.3%, and 4.2% respectively better than the FCM classifier. Fig. 6.4 shows the comparison of the output of MLP, FCM, and softmax classifier.

Table 6.2 Comparison of MSE and SSIM values for different regions of the output of the classifier

Regions	FCM			MLP			Softmax		
	Time required in seconds	MSE	SSIM	Time required in seconds	MSE	SSIM	Time required in seconds	MSE	SSIM
Urban land	16.65	0.0955	0.8882	41.61	0.0053	0.8996	56.26	0.0043	0.9043
Agricultural land	21.25	0.0360	0.8846	51.29	0.0096	0.8986	46.41	0.070	0.9042
Range land	26.71	0.0666	0.8886	67.78	0.0074	0.8992	47.73	0.0054	0.9067
Forest land	29.33	0.0685	0.8844	75.37	0.0068	0.8984	63.42	0.0047	0.9059
Water	36.93	0.0943	0.8885	68.63	0.0074	0.8983	58.10	0.0051	0.9053
Barren land	46.04	0.0349	0.8884	96.14	0.0096	0.8991	102.23	0.0082	0.9036
Unknown region	35.31	0.0295	0.8881	85.31	0.0107	0.8994	91.23	0.0092	0.9029

6.3.1 Comparative study and discussion

Table 6.3 shows the comparison of the proposed methods explained in Chapter 3, Chapter 4, Chapter 5, and chapter 6 with two existing methods described in [15] and [104]. Since double hidden layer with hidden neuron number [20 10] and LMBP Training function gives better results, therefore, the results obtained with these combinations are shown here. From the table 6.3 it was seen that the proposed method described in Chapter 6 gives comparatively better results both in terms of MSE and Accuracy. For the 'Grass' region the performances of the methods discussed in Section 3.2 and 3.3, Section 4.2 and Section 5.2 and that reported in [15] and [104] are best. The best performance of the proposed method Chapter 2 is considered for comparison that is the combination of two hidden layer MLP (20,10). The CAE aided method with softmax produces an MSE of 0.0013 which is 7.1% better than the value obtained with the method discussed in Chapter 5. This is 13.5 times better than that reported in [15] and 12.6 times superior to the results presented in [104]. The corresponding improvement in accuracy is 6.3% and 5.1%. This indicates the advantage of the proposed approach.

Table 6.3 Compare with existing methods

Sl. No.	Methods	MSE	Accuracy in %
1.	MLP + manual labeling	0.0019	92.17
2.	MLP+KMC	0.0018	92.67
3.	SegNet+KMC+MLP	0.0016	93.28
4.	SegNet+KMC+softmax	0.0015	93.46
5.	GAN+MLP	0.0015	95.65
6.	GAN+softmax	0.0014	95.83
7.	CAE+Deeplab-v2+softmax	0.0013	95.91
8.	S. Arumuga Devi et.al.[15]	0.0189	90.21
9.	A. Hassanat et.al [104]	0.0178	91.23

6.4   Conclusion

A deep learning-based method for the extraction of different regions is presented in this work. At first, the high-resolution satellite images are processed with the Contractive Autoencoder (CAE) to remove the noise which is inherently present in the images during acquisition. The output of the CAE is taken as input to train a segmentation network which is a deep neural network. It is seen that the segmentation network when trained with input as the output of CAE gives better results than with input as original images. Finally, the output of the segmentation network is used to train both supervised and unsupervised classifiers to extract different RoIs from the satellite images. A comparison of the results obtained from the classifiers is also presented. Among the classifiers, the softmax classifier gives better results.

From the experimental results it is found that the CAE aided method gives the best results in terms of accuracy and reliability while performing content extraction of satellite images.

7

Conclusion and Future Direction

In this chapter, the summary of findings and the outcomes of the work is presented. Some of the likely future directions are also highlighted in this chapter.

7.1 Summary of Findings

With the advancement of ML and DL techniques and evolving new applications of image processing, the study of various regions of Earth's surface become easier. The design of an efficient system for content extraction of satellite images depends on greater accuracy and the literature survey have indicated the fact that the efficiency of image segmentation techniques can be enhanced by the use of prior knowledge-based methods. However, it is difficult to design a classifier for deriving a proper class/region of satellite images. Therefore, the DL-based methods play an important role in the content extraction of satellite images.

Again, problems with high resolution include the distinct presence of distortion and noise, degradations due to imperfection in the sensors and faulty calibration, etc. Also, limited training data is a familiar problem for high-resolution satellite images as the collection of such images is either expensive or time demanding. Therefore, effective and new strategies to train deep learning-based models are required to overcome these problems. The majority of work carried out in this thesis is related to these issues.

In **Chapter 1** the focus has been to introduce the work, present, and background of the work and highlight the issues related to content extraction of satellite images and methods used for this purpose. The chapter discusses a background related to the content extraction of satellite images. A detailed literature survey related to ML-based, DL-based and adversarial learning-based methods is presented in the chapter. The chapter also presents some of the identified challenges and in the end, the organization of the thesis is described.

Chapter 2 deals with the basic theoretical considerations related to satellite image segmentation and learning-based techniques that help in a better understanding of the present work. Further basic approaches of image segmentation used in the work are also included. Again some of the factors for quality measurement used to describe the performance of the methods are included in the chapter.

In **Chapter 3**, two approaches for content extraction of satellite images are reported. In the first method, a simplified ANN-based approach for the segmentation of satellite images in complex backgrounds is presented. The work considers the formation and training of an ANN in which the pixel values of the various region of the image are used as the target. As this method required manual intervention to select the various region of the image, a second method is reported, where the KMC algorithm is used to label the particular RoI in the image,

Table 7.1 Summary of the proposed method described in Chapter 3

Methods	'Grass' Region		'House' Region		'Sea' region		Advantage
	MSE	Time required in Second	MSE	Time required in Seconds	MSE	Time required in Seconds	
Proposed method	0.0019	90.34	0.0219	92.54	0.0114	82.44	For the grass region the proposed method with KMC is 5.5% better
Proposed method+ KMCA	0.0018	88.24	0.0215	90.14	0.0104	81.35	than the proposed method discussed in section 3.2 in the Chapter 3 in terms of MSE and 9.2 times and
S. Arumuga Devi et.al.[15]	0.0189	136.56	0.0345	178.67	0.0235	157.45	8.8 times better than the results presented in[15] and [104] respectively.
A. Hassanat et.al.[104]	0.0178	156.56	0.0435	189.85	0.0256	169.34	Corresponding improvement in computational time is 54.75% and 77.4%.

and the region is used as the target to train the MLP. From the summary Table 7.1, reported from Chapter 3, the advantage of the proposed system is clearly visible. Our proposed system shows a lower MSE value than the system reported by the authors in [15] and [104].

Chapter 4 is related to the design of a method for semantic segmentation based on deep learning in satellite images is discussed. The method comprises of the training and formation of a SegNet where the input images are satellite images. In the work, the target to the network was taken from the output of KMCA with their label of the required RoI. Then, with the output of the SegNet as input and the pixel values of various RoI as the target, a neuro-computing structure is trained to segment the various RoI. From the summary Table 7.2, reported from Chapter 4, the advantage of the proposed system is clearly visible. Our proposed system shows a lower MSE value than the system reported by the authors in [15] and [104].

Chapter 5 describes the implementation of a semi-supervised adversarial learning method to extract different RoIs of satellite images. The method deals with the problem of extraction of meaningful content from satellite images using learning-based approaches with the limited availability of appropriate prior information. In the proposed method, in addition to unlabeled data, some supervision is also adopted to train a composite network. It consists of two learning-based networks used for segmentation and discrimination which are trained

Table 7.2 Summary of the proposed method described in Chapter 4

Methods	'Grass' Region		'House' Region		'Sea' region		Advantage
	MSE	Time required in Seconds	MSE	Time required in Seconds	MSE	Time required in Seconds	
Proposed method	0.0019	90.34	0.0219	92.54	0.0114	82.44	For the grass region the proposed method with SegNet is 12.5% better
Proposed method+ KMCA	0.0018	88.24	0.0215	90.14	0.0104	81.35	than the proposed method discussed in section 3.3 in the Chapter 3 in terms of MSE and 10.8
Proposed method+ SegNeT	0.0016	101.64	0.0213	150.67	0.0098	147.67	times better than the method in and 10.12 times superior [15] to the method [104]
S. Arumuga Devi et.al.[15]	0.0189	136.56	0.0345	178.67	0.0235	157.45	
A. Hassanat et.al.[104]	0.0178	156.56	0.0435	189.85	0.0256	169.34	

Table 7.3 Summary of the proposed method described in Chapter 5

Sl. No.	Methods	MSE	Accuracy in %	Advantage
1.	MLP + manual labeling	0.0019	92.17	The proposed method with GAN produces MSE
2.	MLP+KMC	0.0018	92.67	of 0.0014 which is 14.2% better than
3.	SegNet+KMC+MLP	0.0016	93.28	the value obtained with the method discussed
4.	SegNet+KMC+softmax	0.0015	93.46	in Chapter 4. This is 12.5 times better than
5.	GAN+MLP	0.0015	95.65	that reported in [15] and 11.7 times
6.	GAN+softmax	0.0014	95.83	superior to the results presented in [104].
7.	S. Arumuga Devi et.al.[15]	0.0189	90.21	Corresponding improvement in accuracy
8	A. Hassanat et.al [104]	0.0178	91.23	is 5.8% and 4.8%

with the adversarial algorithm. The algorithm being semi-supervised uses both labeled and unlabeled data for generating better results. Finally, the outputs of the segmentation network are used as input to train a classifier to extract the region RoIs of the satellite images. The classifier used is MLP (supervised), softmax (supervised), SVM (supervised), KNN (supervised), SOM (unsupervised), PNN (unsupervised), and FCM (unsupervised). From the summary Table 7.3, reported from Chapter 5, the advantage of the proposed system is clearly visible. Our proposed system shows a lower MSE value than the system reported by the authors in [15] and [104].

In **Chapter 6** a Contractive Autoencoder aided deep learning-based approach is reported to extract different RoIs of satellite images. The method deals with the problem of high-resolution satellite images which may contain noise during acquisition that affects the performance of the segmentation process. a deep learning-based method to extract different regions of interest(RoIs)is presented in which a DL based noise removal process from the input high-resolution satellite images is also included. In the work, at first, the high-resolution satellite images are processed with the Contractive Autoencoder (CAE) to remove the noise which is inherently present in the images during acquisition. The output of the CAE is taken as input to train a segmentation network which is a deep neural network. Finally, the output of the segmentation network is used to train both supervised and unsupervised classifiers to extract different RoIs from the satellite images. From the summary Table 7.4, reported from Chapter 6, the advantage of the proposed system is clearly visible. Our proposed system shows a lower MSE value than the system reported by the authors in [15] and [104].

Table 7.4 Summary of the proposed method described in Chapter 6

Sl. No.	Methods	MSE	Accuracy in %	Advantage
1.	MLP + manual labeling	0.0019	92.17	The CAE aided method with softmax produces MSE
2.	MLP+KMC	0.0018	92.67	of 0.0013 which is 7.1% better than
3.	SegNet+KMC+MLP	0.0016	93.28	the value obtained with the method discussed
4.	SegNet+KMC+softmax	0.0015	93.46	in Chapter 5. This is 13.5 times better than
5.	GAN+MLP	0.0015	95.65	that reported in [15] and 12.6 times
6.	GAN+softmax	0.0014	95.83	superior to the results presented in [104].
7.	CAE+Deeplab-v2+softmax	0.0013	95.91	Corresponding improvement in accuracy
8.	S. Arumuga Devi et.al.[15]	0.0189	90.21	is 6.3% and 5.1%
9.	A. Hassanat et.al [104]	0.0178	91.23	

7.2 Limitations

The primary limitations can be listed as-

- In designing of the classifier for content extraction of satellite images there is no specific rule for determining the structure of ANN. To determine the appropriate structure of the ANN trial and error method is adopted.

- In DL-based methods, the training of DNNs requires annotated data. If the annotation is not properly done then it will affect the accuracy of the method.

- With the use of conventional CPUs for implementing the learning-based approaches, training latency is a marked limitation that has been noted in relevant chapters.

7.3 Future Direction

Despite certain limitations in the form of the limited annotated dataset, scope to increase the accuracy and training latency, the following may be considered as the future directions of the work.

- To develop the method so that the computation time can be reduced especially with the use of specified hardware and graphical processing unit (GPU) based processing.

- To develop an unsupervised method with better accuracy since the annotated visual data is difficult to obtain for satellite images.

References

[1] T.Blaschke, *Object based image analysis for remote sensing*, International Journal of Geo-Information. vol.65, pp. 2-16, 2010.

[2] E.F. Salma, E.H. Mohammed, R. Mohamed, M. Mohamed, *A Hybrid Feature Extraction for Satellite Image Segmentation Using Statistical Global and Local Feature*, in Proceedings of the Mediterranean Conference on Information and Communication Technologies, Lecture Notes in Electrical Engineering, vol 380. Springer, Cham, pp. 23-78, 2016.

[3] W. X. OrcID, Y.Z. Zhang, J. Liu, L. Luo and K. Yang, *Road Extraction from High Resolution Image with Deep Convolution Network-A Case Study of GF-2 Image* Proceedings of International Electronic Conference on Remote Sensing, vol.2, no.7, 2018.

[4] K. Y. Win, S. Choomchuay, K. Hamamoto and M. Raveesunthornkiat, "Artificial neural network based nuclei segmentation on cytology pleural effusion images," 2017 International Conference on Intelligent Informatics and Biomedical Sciences (ICIIBMS), Okinawa, pp. 245-249, 2017.

[5] J. S. Sevak , A. D. Kapadia, J. B. Chavda, A. Shah and M. Rahevar *Survey on semantic image segmentation techniques*, International Conference on Intelligent Sustainable Systems (ICISS), Palladam, pp. 306-313, 2017.

[6] J. Shotton, M. Johnson, R. Cipolla, *Semantic Texton Forests for Image Categorization and Segmentation*, in Proceedings of IEEE Conference on Computer Vision and pattern Recognition, pp. 1-6, Anchorage, AK, USA, 2008.

[7] X. Lin , X. Wang and W. Cui, *An Automatic Image Segmentation Algorithm Based on Spiking Neural Network Model*, in Proceedings of International Conference on Intelligent Computing, Sringer, pp. 248-258, Taiyuan, China, 2014.

[8] V. Badrinarayanan, A. Kendall, R. Cipolla *SegNet: A Deep Convolutional Encoder-Decoder Architecture for Image Segmentation*, IEEE Transactions on Pattern Analysis and Machine Intelligence , vol-39, pp. 2481 - 2495, 2017.

[9] J. Shotton, A. Fitzgibbon, M. Cook, T. Sharp, M. Finocchio, R. Moore, A. Kipman, A. Blake, *Real-Time Human Pose Recognition in Parts from Single Depth Images*, in CPVR, pp. 1-8, Colorado Springs, CO, USA, 2016.

[10] A. Krizhevsky, I. Sutskever, G. Hinton, *Imagenet classification with deep convolutional neural networks*, Advances in Neural Information Processing Systems, vol.2, no. 7, pp. 1-7, 2012.

[11] X. Chen, S. Xiang, C. Liu, C. Pan *Vehicle Detection in Satellite Images by Parallel Deep Convolutional Neural Networks*, 2nd IAPR Asian Conference on Pattern Recognition (ACPR),Taiyuan, China, pp. 181-185, 2013.

[12] L. Zhu, Y. Chen, P. Ghamisi and J. A. Benediktsson,*Generative Adversarial Networks for Hyperspectral Image Classification*,IEEE Transaction on Geoscience and Remote Sensing, vol. 56, no. 9, pp. 5046-5062, 2018.

[13] I. Goodfellow, Y. Bengio and A. Courville, *Deep Learning (Adaptive Computation and Machine Learning series)*, Regularization for Deep Learning, Deep Learning, The MIT Press, pp. 145-245, 2016.

[14] B. Stojanovic, A. Neskovic, Z. Popovic and V. Lukic, "*ANN based fingerprint image ROI segmentation*", in Proceedings of 22nd Telecommunications Forum Telfor (TELFOR), pp. 1-6, Belgrade, Serbia, 2014.

[15] S. Arumugadevi and V. Seenivasagam, *Color image segmentation using feedforward neural networks with FCM*, in International Journal of Automation and Computing, Springer, Vol. 13, N0. 5, pp. 491-500, 2016.

[16] H. Zhu and J. Qi, "Using Genetic neural networks in image segmentation researching", in Proceedings of IEEE Intrnational Conference on Multimedia Technology (ICMT), pp. 1-6, Hangzhou, China, 2011.

[17] S. A. Hannan, R. R. Manza and R. J. Ramteke, *Generalized Regression Neural Network and Radial Basis Function for Heart Disease Diagnosis*, International Journal of Computer Applications, vol. 7, no.13, pp. 7-13. 2010.

[18] P. Upadhyay and J. K. Chhabra, *Modified Self Organizing Feature Map Neural Network (MSOFM NN) Based Gray Image Segmentation*, in Transaction of 11th International Conference on Information Processing, Science Direct, vol. 54 pp. 671-675, 2015.

[19] C. Wang, S. Li, K. He, Z. Lin and C. Jiang, *Automatic Image Segmentation Using Pulse Coupled Neural Network and Independent Component Analysis*, in Proceedings of IEEE International Conference on Machine Vision and Human-Machine Interface (MVHI), pp. 1-6, Kaifeng, China, 2010.

[20] W. Xinchun, Y. Qing, Y. Kaihu, L. Running and S. Kangyun, *A new image segmentation algorithm based on PCNN and Maximal Correlative Criterion*, in Proceedings of 10th IEEE International Conference on Signal Processing (ICSP), pp. 1-6, Beijing, China, 2010.

[21] T. Si, A. De and A. K. Bhattacharjee, *Artificial Neural Network based Lesion Segmentation of Brain MRI*, in Communications on Applied Electronics, Published by Foundation of Computer Science (FCS), NY, USA, vol. 4 no.5 pp.1-5, 2016.

[22] M. J. Moghaddam and H. S. Zadeh, *Medical Image Segmentation Using Artificial Neural Networks*, Chapter 6, Artificial Neural Networks - Methodological Advances and Biomedical Applications, pp. 121-138, 2011.

[23] F. Cao, J. Lu , J. Chu, Z. Zhou, J. Zhao and G. Chen, *Leukocyte image segmentation using feed forward neural networks with random weights*, in Proceedings of 11th International Conference on Natural Computation (ICNC), pp. 29-51, Zhangjiajie, China, 2015.

[24] K. Sharma T., S. Babu N.S., Y.N. Mamatha, Satellite Image Feature Extraction Using Neural Network Technique. In: Kumar M. A., R. S., Kumar T. (eds) Proceedings of International Conference on Advances in Computing. Advances in Intelligent Systems and Computing, vol 174, pp.1-6, Springer, New Delhi, 2013.

[25] K. M. Buddhiraju and I. A. Rizvi, "Comparison of CBF, ANN and SVM classifiers for object based classification of high resolution satellite images" 2010 IEEE International Geoscience and Remote Sensing Symposium, pp. 40-43, Honolulu, HI, 2010, .

[26] A. Mukhopadhyay, S. Bandyopadhyay and U. Maulik, "Combining multiobjective fuzzy clustering and probabilistic ANN classifier for unsupervised pattern classification: Application to satellite image segmentation," in Procedings of 2008 IEEE Congress on Evolutionary Computation (IEEE World Congress on Computational Intelligence), Hong Kong, pp. 877-883, 2008.

[27] S. U. Indira and A. C. Ramesh, "Image Segmentation Using Artificial Neural Network and Genetic Algorithm: A Comparative Analysis", in Proceedings of 2011 International Conference on Process Automation, Control and Computing, Coimbatore, pp. 1-6, 2011.

[28] X. Du, Y. Li and D. Yao, "A Support Vector Machine Based Algorithm for Magnetic Resonance Image Segmentation," in Proceedings of 2008 Fourth International Conference on Natural Computation, Jinan, pp. 49-53, 2008, .

[29] X. Wang, S. Wang, Y. Zhu and X. Meng, "Image segmentation based on Support Vector Machine," in Proceedings of 2nd International Conference on Computer Science and Network Technology, Changchun, pp. 202-206, 2012.

[30] N. Abdullah, U. K. Ngah and S. A. Aziz, "Image classification of brain MRI using support vector machine," in Proceedings of IEEE International Conference on Imaging Systems and Techniques, Penang, pp. 242-247, 2011.

[31] L. Zhang, F. Lin and B. Zhang, "Support vector machine learning for image retrieval," in Proceedings of International Conference on Image Processing (Cat. No.01CH37205),pp. 721-724 vol.2, Thessaloniki, Greece, 2001.

[32] E. P. Giri and A. M. Arymurthy, "Quantitative evaluation for simple segmentation SVM in landscape image," in Proceeding of International Conference on Advanced Computer Science and Information System, pp. 369-374, Jakarta, 2014.

[33] J. Zhang, L. Liu, D. Huang, X. Fu and Q. Huang, "Clothing Co-Segmentation Based on HOG Features and E-SVM Classifier," in Proceedings of 6th International Conference on Digital Home (ICDH),pp. 39-74, Guangzhou, 2016, .

[34] N. Nagoda and L. Ranathunga, "Rice Sample Segmentation and Classification Using Image Processing and Support Vector Machine," in Proceedings of IEEE 13th International Conference on Industrial and Information Systems (ICIIS), pp. 179-184, Rupnagar, India, 2018.

[35] S. Zhao, X. Hao and X. Li, "Segmentation of Fingerprint Images Using Support Vector Machines," in Proceedings of Second International Symposium on Intelligent Information Technology Application, pp. 423-427, Shanghai, 2008.

[36] T. Liu, X. Wen, J. Quan and X. Xu, "Multiscale SAR Image Segmentation Using Support Vector Machines," in Proceedings of Congress on Image and Signal Processing, pp. 706-709, Sanya, Hainan, 2008.

[37] S.W. Baik, S.M. Ahn, J.W. Lee, K.K. Win, *Adaptive Segmentation of Remote-Sensing Images for Aerial Surveillance* In: Petkov N., Westenberg M.A. (eds) Computer Analysis of Images and Patterns, CAIP 2003. Lecture Notes in Computer Science, vol 2756. Springer, Berlin, Heidelberg, 2003.

[38] W. Lu, W. Sun, J.W. Huang and H.T. Lu, "Digital image forensics using statistical features and neural network classifier," in Proceedings of International Conference on Machine Learning and Cybernetics, pp. 2831-2834, Kunming, 2008. .

[39] J. K. Sing, D. K. Basu, M. Nasipuri and M. Kundu, "Self-adaptive RBF neural network-based segmentation of medical images of the brain," in Proceedings of 2005 International Conference on Intelligent Sensing and Information Processing, pp. 447-452, Chennai, India, 2005, .

[40] C.Y. Chang and S.Y. Fu, "Image Classification using a Module RBF Neural Network," in Proceedings of First International Conference on Innovative Computing, Information and Control vol.1, pp. 270-273, Beijing, 2006, .

[41] D. Kovacevic and S. Loncaric, "Radial basis function-based image segmentation using a receptive field," in Proceedings of Computer Based Medical Systems, Maribor,pp. 126-130, Slovenia, 1997, .

[42] Y. Chen, "Microscopic Image Segementing and Classification with RBF Neural Network", in Proceedings of Fourth International Symposium on Information Science and Engineering, pp. 311-314, Shanghai, 2012.

[43] A. S. Parihar, "Satellite image segmentation based on differential evolution", in Proceedings of International Conference on Intelligent Sustainable Systems (ICISS), pp. 621-624, Palladam, 2017.

[44] S. Ghassemi et al., "Satellite Image Segmentation with Deep Residual Architectures for Time-Critical Applications," in Proceedings of 26th European Signal Processing Conference (EUSIPCO), pp. 2235-2239, Rome, 2018.

[45] J. Long , E. Shelhamer, and T. Darrell, *Fully convolutional networks for semantic segmentation*, in Proceedings of IEEE Conference on Computer Vision and Pattern Recognition (CVPR), pp. 3431-3440, Boston, MA, 2015.

[46] C. Szegedy, W. Liu , Y. Jia , P. Sermanet , S. Reed , D. Anguelov , D. Erhan , V. Vanhoucke , and A. Rabinovich *Going deeper with convolutions*, in Proceedings of International Conference on Intelligent Sustainable Systems (ICISS), pp. 621-624, Palladam, 2014.

[47] J. Donahue, Y. Jia, O. Vinyals, J. Hoffman, N. Zhang , E. Tzeng , and T. Darrell, *DeCAF: A deep convolutional activation feature for generic visual recognition*, in Proceedings of IEEE Conference on Computer Vision and Pattern Recognition (CVPR), pp. 3431-3440, Boston, MA, 2014.

[48] O. Ronneberger , P. Fischer , T. Brox, *U-Net: Convolutional Networks for Biomedical Image Segmentation*, in Proceedings of Fourth International Symposium on Information Science and Engineering, Computer Science Department and BIOSS Centre for Biological Signalling Studies, University of Freiburg, Germany, 2015.

[49] A. Yoshihara , T. Takiguchi , and Y. Ariki, *Feature extraction and classification of multispectral imagery by using convolutional neural network.* In Proceedings of International Workshop on Frontiers of Computer Vision, pp. 3431-3440, Boston, MA, 2017.

[50] S. Jegou, M. Drozdzal , D. Vazquez , A. Romero , Y. Bengio,*The One Hundred Layers Tiramisu:Fully Convolutional DenseNets for Semantic Segmentation*, in Proceedings of IEEE Conference on Computer Vision and Pattern Recognition (CVPR), pp. 3431-3440, Boston, MA, 2015.

[51] J. Patravali , S. Jain , S. Chilamkurthy ,*2D-3D Fully Convolutional Neural Networks for Cardiac MR Segmentation.* In proceedings of Statistical Atlases and Computational Models of the Heart. ACDC and MMWHS Challenges. STACOM 2017. Lecture Notes in Computer Science, vol 10663. Springer, Cham, 2018.

[52] M. Langkvist, A. Kiselev, M. Alirezaie, A. Loutfi, *Classification and Segmentation of Satellite Orthoimagery Using Convolutional Neural Networks*, Remote Sens. ,vol 8,no. 329, pp. 124- 135, 2016.

[53] G. Huang , Z. Liu , K. Q. Weinberger , and L. V. Maaten . *Densely connected convolutional networks*, in Proceedings of International Conference on Intelligent Sustainable Systems (ICISS), pp. 621-624, Palladam, 2014.

[54] A. Chaurasia , E. Culurciello, *LinkNet: Exploiting Encoder Representations for Efficient Semantic Segmentation*, in Proceedings of IEEE Conference on Computer Vision and Pattern Recognition (CVPR), pp. 3431-3440, Boston, MA, 2015. 2017.

[55] K. He, X. Zhang, S. Ren, and J. Sun, *Deep residual learning for image recognition*, in Proceedings of IEEE Conference on Computer Vision and Pattern Recognition (CVPR), pp. 3431-3440, Boston, MA, 2017.

[56] H. Zhao, J. Shi, X. Qi, X, Wang, J. Jia *Pyramid Scene Parsing Network*, in Proceedings of International Conference on Intelligent Sustainable Systems (ICISS), pp. 621-624, Palladam, 2016.

[57] K. Jagannath, K. Jadhav ,R. P. Singh *Automatic semantic segmentation and classification of remote sensing data for agriculture* in Mathematical Models in Engineering, vol. 4, no. 2, p. 112-137, 2018, .

[58] S. Ghassemi, and E. MagliOrcID, *Convolutional Neural Networks for On-Board Cloud Screening*, Remote Sens. vol. 11 no.12, pp. 1417-1456,2019,

[59] H. Liu, H. Du, D.Zeng, J. Compututer Science and Technology. *SVM Pixel Classification on Colour Image Segmentation* in Proceedings of International Conference on Intelligent Sustainable Systems (ICISS), pp. 621-624, Palladam, 2019,

[60] M. Wurma, T. Starkb, X. X. Zhubc,M. Weigandad, H. Taubenbocka, Semantic segmentation of slums in satellite images using transfer learning on fully convolutional neural networks, ISPRS Journal of Photogrammetry and Remote Sensing, Elsevier. vol. 150, pp. 59-69 April 2019,

[61] G. Morales, A. Ramirez and J. Telles, *End-to-end Cloud Segmentation in High-Resolution Multispectral Satellite Imagery Using Deep Learning*, 2019 IEEE XXVI International Conference on Electronics, Electrical Engineering and Computing (INTERCON), pp. 1-4., Lima, Peru, 2019.

[62] C. Henry, S. M. Azimi and N. Merkle,*Road Segmentation in SAR Satellite Images With Deep Fully Convolutional Neural Networks*, in IEEE Geoscience and Remote Sensing Letters, vol. 15, no. 12, pp. 1867-1871, Dec. 2018.

[63] S. Ghassemi, A. Fiandrotti, G. Francini and E. Magli, *Learning and Adapting Robust Features for Satellite Image Segmentation on Heterogeneous Data Sets*, in IEEE Transactions on Geoscience and Remote Sensing, vol. 57, no. 9, pp. 6517-6529, Sept. 2019.

[64] T. Selea and M. Neagul, "Using Deep Networks for Semantic Segmentation of Satellite Images," in Proceedings of 19th International Symposium on Symbolic and Numeric Algorithms for Scientific Computing (SYNASC), Timisoara, pp. 409-415, 2017.

[65] M. Wu , C. Zhang , J. Liu, L. Zhou, AND X. Li *Towards Accurate High Resolution Satellite Image Semantic Segmentation*,IEEE Transactions on Geoscience and Remote Sensing, vol. 57, no. 9, pp. 6517-6529, Sept. 2019.

[66] H. Tao, W. Li, X. Qin and D. Jia, *Image semantic segmentation based on convolutional neural network and conditional random field*, in Proceedings of Tenth International Conference on Advanced Computational Intelligence (ICACI), pp. 568-572, Xiamen, 2018, .

[67] S. Sunetci and H. F. Ates, *Semantic image segmentation with deep features*, in Proceedings of 26th Signal Processing and Communications Applications Conference (SIU), Izmir, pp.1-6, 2018.

[68] G. Wang et al., *Interactive Medical Image Segmentation Using Deep Learning With Image-Specific Fine Tuning*, in IEEE Transactions on Medical Imaging, vol. 37, no. 7, pp. 1562-1573, July, 2018.

[69] P. Luo, G. Wang, L. Lin and X. Wang, *Deep Dual Learning for Semantic Image Segmentation*, in Proceedings of IEEE International Conference on Computer Vision (ICCV), Venice, pp. 2737-2745, 2017, .

[70] D. Liao, H. Lu, X. Xu and Q. Gao, *Image Segmentation Based on Deep Learning Features*, in Proceedings of Eleventh International Conference on Advanced Computational Intelligence (ICACI),pp. 296-301, Guilin, China, 2019,

[71] Z. Kong, T. Li, J. Luo and S. Xu *Automatic Tissue Image Segmentation Based on Image Processing and Deep Learning* Journal of Healthcare Engineering, vol.6, pp.8-16, 2019,

[72] C. Wang, L. Mauch, Z. Guo and B. Yang, *On semantic image segmentation using deep convolutional neural network with shortcuts and easy class extension,* in Proceedings of Sixth International Conference on Image Processing Theory, Tools and Applications (IPTA), pp. 1-6, Oulu, 2016.

[73] Z. Guo, X. Li, H. Huang, N. Guo and Q. Li, *Deep Learning-Based Image Segmentation on Multimodal Medical Imaging*, in IEEE Transactions on Radiation and Plasma Medical Sciences, vol. 3, no. 2, pp. 162-169, March, 2019.

[74] M.H. Hesamian, W. Jia, *Deep Learning Techniques for Medical Image Segmentation: Achievements and Challenges*, Journal of Digital Imaging, vol.32, no.582. pp.1-6, 2019.

[75] Y. Duan, X. Tao, C. Han, X. Qin and J. Lu, *Multi-Scale Convolutional Neural Network for SAR Image Semantic Segmentation*, in Proceedings of IEEE Global Communications Conference (GLOBECOM), Abu Dhabi, United Arab Emirates, pp. 1-6, 2018.

[76] D. R. Lucio, R. Laroca, E. Severo, A. S. Britto and D. Menotti, *Fully Convolutional Networks and Generative Adversarial Networks Applied to Sclera Segmentation*, in Proceedings of IEEE 9th International Conference on Biometrics Theory, Applications and Systems (BTAS), Redondo Beach, CA, USA, pp. 1-7, 2018.

[77] C. Zhang , *MS-GAN: GAN-Based Semantic Segmentation of Multiple Sclerosis Lesions in Brain Magnetic Resonance Imaging*,in Proceedings of Digital Image Computing: Techniques and Applications (DICTA), Canberra, Australia, pp. 1-8, 2018, .

[78] Y. LI AND L. SHEN, *cC-GAN: A Robust Transfer-Learning Framework for HEp-2 Specimen Image Segmentation*, in Proceedings of IEEE Global Communications Conference (GLOBECOM), Abu Dhabi, United Arab Emirates, pp. 1-6, 2018.

[79] S. Roy, E. Sangineto, N. Sebe and B. Demir, "Semantic-Fusion Gans for Semi-Supervised Satellite Image Classification," in Proceedings of 25th IEEE International Conference on Image Processing (ICIP), Athens, pp. 684-688, 2018,.

[80] Q. Shi, X. Liu, X. Li *Road Detection From Remote Sensing Images by Generative Adversarial Networks*, in IEEE Transactions on Radiation and Plasma Medical Sciences, vol. 3, no. 2, pp. 162-169, March, 2019.

[81] M. Bosch, C. M. Gifford and P. A. *Rodriguez,Super-Resolution for Overhead Imagery Using DenseNets and Adversarial Learning* ,in Proceedings of IEEE Winter Conference on Applications of Computer Vision (WACV), Lake Tahoe, NV, 2018, pp. 1414-1422.

[82] Y. Shi, Q. Li and X. X. Zhu, *Building Footprint Generation Using Improved Generative Adversarial Networks,* in IEEE Geoscience and Remote Sensing Letters, vol. 16, no. 4, pp. 603-607, April 2019.

[83] 201 E. Collier, *Progressively Growing Generative Adversarial Networks for High Resolution Semantic Segmentation of Satellite Images,* in Proceedings of IEEE International Conference on Data Mining Workshops (ICDMW), pp. 763-769, Singapore, Singapore, 2018,

[84] X. Hu, X. Zhao, K. Huang and T. Tan, "Adversarial Learning Based Saliency Detection," in Proceedings of IEEE 4th IAPR Asian Conference on Pattern Recognition (ACPR), Nanjing, pp. 256-261, 2017, .

[85] S. Qiu, Y. Zhao, J. Jiao, Y. Wei and S. Wei, *Referring Image Segmentation by Generative Adversarial Learning,* in IEEE Transactions on Multimedia, vol. 16, no. 4, pp. 603-607, 2017.

[86] L. Huang, C. Bai, Y. Lu, S. Chen and Q. Tian, *Adversarial Learning for Content-Based Image Retrieval,* in Proceedings of IEEE Conference on Multimedia Information Processing and Retrieval (MIPR), pp. 97-102, San Jose, CA, USA, 2019.

[87] R. Kaur , D. Sharma, *A Review of Various Categories of Satellite Image Processing in Remote Sensing.* In: Singh R., Choudhury S., Gehlot A. (eds) Intelligent Communication, Control and Devices. Advances in Intelligent Systems and Computing, vol 624, pp,10-16 Springer, Singapore, 2018.

[88] J. Yang, P. Li, Y. He, *A multi-band approach to unsupervised scale parameter selection for multi-scale image segmentation,* in Multimedia Information Processing and Retrieval (MIPR), vol. 6, pp,10-16, Elsevier, August, 2014.

[89] J. Liu, P. Li , X. Wang, *A new segmentation method for very high resolution imagery using spectral and morphological information,* Multimedia Information Processing and Retrieval (MIPR), vol. 5, pp,25-36, Elsevier, March 2015.

[90] Z. Huang, J. Zhang, F. Xu, *A novel multi-scale relative salience feature for remote sensing image analysis,* Multimedia Information Processing and Retrieval (MIPR), vol. 4, pp,67-86, Elsevier, January 2014.

[91] Z. Wang, J. R. Jensen, J. Im, *An automatic region-based image segmentation algorithm for remote sensing applications,* Multimedia Information Processing and Retrieval (MIPR), vol.1, pp,7-9, Elsevier, October 2010.

[92] H. Xie, S. Wang, K. Liu, S. Lin, and B. Hou, *Multilayer feature learning for polarimetric synthetic radar data classification,* in Proceedings of IEEE International Geoscience and Remote Sensing Symposium (IGARSS), pp. 7-12, 2014.

[93] J. Geng, J. Fan, H. Wang, X. Ma, B. Li, and F. Chen, *High-resolution SAR image classification via deep convolutional autoencoders,* in IEEE Geoscience and Remote Sensing Letters, vol. 12, no. 11, pp. 2351- 2355, 2015.

[94] J. Geng, H. Wang, J. Fan, and X. Ma, *Deep supervised and contractive neural network for SAR image classification*, IEEE Transactions on Geoscience and Remote Sensing, vol. 55, no. 4, pp. 2442- 2459, 2017.

[95] Y. Liu,D. Nguyen, N. Deligiannis, W. Ding, A. Munteanu, *Hourglass-ShapeNetwork Based Semantic Segmentation for High Resolution Aerial Imagery.* in Remote Sensing Letters., vol. 9, no. 522, pp. 40-57, 2017.

[96] R. Yasrab, N. Gu, X. Zhang, *An Encoder-Decoder Based Convolution Neural Network (CNN) for Future Advanced Driver Assistance System (ADAS).* in proceedings of International conference on signal processing and integrated networks, pp 56- 89, 2017.

[97] M. Barthakur and K.K. Sarma, *Complex Image Segmentation using K-means Clustering Aided Neuro-computing*, in proceedings of 5th IEEE International Conference on Signal Processing and Integrated Networks (SPIN), Noida, New Delhi, Feb.,2018.

[98] R. C. Gonzalez, R. E. Woods, *Digital Image Processing*, 4th Edition, New Delhi, Pearson, 2018.

[99] D. Patra, M. K. Das and S. Pradhan,*Integration of FCM, PCA and Neural Networks for Classification of ECG Arrhythmias* IAENG International Journal of Computer Science, vol.36, No.3, pp.3-8, 2010.

[100] S. Rifai, P. Vincent, X. Muller, X. Glorot and Y. Bengio, *Contractive Auto-Encoders: Explicit Invariance during Feature Extraction*, in Proceedings of International Conference on Machine Learning, pp. 833-840, Washington, USA, 2011.

[101] X. Lin, X. Wang and W. Cui, *An Automatic Image Segmentation Algorithm Based on Spiking Neural Network Model*, in Proceedings of International Conference on Intelligent Computing, Sringer, pp. 248-258, Taiyuan, China, 2014.

[102] United States Geological Survey https://earthexplorer.usgs.gov/

[103] S. Haykin, *Neural Networks A Comprehensive Foundation*, 2nd edn. Pearson Education, New Delhi, 2003.

[104] A. Hassanat and M. Alkasassbeh, *Colour-based Lips Segmentation Method using Artificial Neural Networks* in Proceedings of 6th IEEE International Conference on Information and Communication Systems (ICICS), pp. 188-193, Amman, Jordan, 2015.

[105] M. Barthakur, K. K. Sarma and N. Mastorakis, *Learning Aided Structures for Image Segmentation in Complex Background*, IEEE European Conference on Electrical Engineering and Computer Science (EECS 2017), Bern, Switzerland, Nov., 2017.

[106] M. Barthakur, K. K. Sarma and N. Mastorakis, *Neural Network methods for Image Segmentation*, In Applied Physics, System Science and Computers II, APSAC Lecture Notes in Electrical Engineering, vol. 489. Springer, Cham, 2019

[107] E. Maggiori, Y. Tarabalka, G. Charpiat and P. Alliez, *Can semantic labeling methods generalize to any city? the inria aerial image labeling benchmark*, IEEE International Geoscience and Remote Sensing Symposium (IGARSS), pp. 3226-3229, Fort Worth, TX, 2017.

[108] I. Demir, K. Koperski, D. Lindenbaum, G. Pang, J. Huang, S. Basu, F. Hughes, D. Tuia and R. Raskar, *DeepGlobe 2018: A Challenge to Parse the Earth through Satellite Images*, Computer Vision and Pattern Recognition, pp.8-9, 2018.

[109] Q. Jiang, L. Cao , M. Cheng , C. Wang and J. Li, *Deep neural networks-based vehicle detection in satellite images*, In International Symposium on Bioelectronics and Bioinformatics (ISBB), pp. 184-187, Beijing, 2015.

[110] T. Blaschke, *Object based image analysis for remote sensing*, Multimedia Information Processing and Retrieval (MIPR), vol. 1, pp.2-16, 2010.

[111] L.C. Chen, G. Papandreou, I. Kokkinos, K. Murphy, and A. L.Yuille. *Deeplab: Semantic image segmentation with deep convolutional nets, atrous convolution, and fully connected crfs*, in IEEE Transactions on Pattern Analysis and Machine Intelligence, vol. 5, pp. 40-55, 2017.

[112] M. Barthakur and K.K. Sarma, *Semantic Segmentation using K-means Clustering and Deep Learning in Satellite Image*, in Proceedings of 2nd IEEE International Conference on Innovations in Electronics, Signal Processing and Communication (IESC 2019), Shillong, Meghalaya, March, 2019.

[113] M. Barthakur and K.K. Sarma, *Deep Learning Based Semantic Segmentation Applied to Satellite Image*, In Data Visualization and Knowledge Engineering. Lecture Notes on Data Engineering and Communications Technologies, vol 32. pp. 17- 57, Springer, Cham, 2019.

[114] K. Simonyan, A. Zisserman, *Very Deep Convolutional Networks for Large-Scale Image Recognition*, IEEE International Geoscience and Remote Sensing Symposium (IGARSS), pp. 3226-3229, Fort Worth, TX, 2014..

[115] K. He, X. Zhang, S. Ren, J. Sun, *Deep residual learning for image recognition*, in Proceedings of the IEEE Conference on Computer Vision and Pattern Recognition, pp. 770-778, 2016.

[116] R. Girshick, J. Donahue, T. Darrell, J. Malik *Rich feature hierarchies for accurate object detection and semantic segmentation*, in Proceedings of the IEEE Conference on Computer Vision and Pattern Recognition, pp. 77-98, 2014.

[117] B. Benjdira, Y. Bazi, A. Koubaa and K. Ouni, *Unsupervised Domain Adaptation Using Generative Adversarial Networks for Semantic Segmentation of Aerial Images*, Remote Sens., vol.11, No.1369, 2019.

[118] P. Luc, C. Couprie, S. Chintala and J. Verbeek, *Semantic Segmentation using Adversarial Networks*, in Proceedings of NIPS Workshop on Adversarial Training, Barcelona, Spain, pp.1-6, 2016.

[119] N. Souly, C. Spampinato and M. Shah, *Semi Supervised Semantic Segmentation Using Generative Adversarial Network*, in Proceedings of IEEE International Conference on Computer Vision (ICCV), pp.1-7, Venice, Italy, 2017.

[120] W.C. Hung, Y.H. Tsai, Y.T. Liou, Y.Y. Lin and M.H. Yang, *Adversarial Learning for Semi-Supervised Semantic Segmentation*, Computer Vision and Pattern Recognition, vol. 6, pp. 1-23, 2018.

[121] H. Valpola, *From neural pca to deep unsupervised learning*, Advances in Independent Component Analysis and Learning Machines, vol. 7 no.4, pp. 143-171, 2015.

[122] L.C. Chen, G. Papandreou, I. Kokkinos, K. Murphy, and A. L.Yuille. *Deeplab: Semantic image segmentation with deep convolutional nets, atrous convolution, and fully connected crfs*. In TPAMI, 2017.

[123] F. Yu and V. Koltun, *Multi-scale context aggregation by dilated convolutions*,in Proceedings of IEEE International Conference on Computer Vision (ICCV), pp.1-7, Venice, Italy, 2016..

[124] A. L. Maas, A. Y. Hannun, and A. Y. Ng. *Rectifier nonlinearities improve neural network acoustic models* IComputer Vision and Pattern Recognition, vol. 6, pp. 1-23, 2013.

[125] J. Hoffman, E. Tzeng, T. Park, J.Y. Zhu, P. Isola, K. Saenko, A. A. Efros and Trevor Darrell, *Cycada: Cycle consistent adversarial domain adaptation*, in Proceedings of the IEEE Conference on Computer Vision and Pattern Recognition, pp. 77-98, 2014.

[126] D. K. and J. Ba. *Adam: A method for stochastic optimization*. in Proceedings of the IEEE Conference on Computer Vision and Pattern Recognition, pp. 77-98, 2014.

[127] G. Cheng, Z. Li, J. Han, X. Yao and L. Guo, *Exploring Hierarchical Convolutional Features for Hyperspectral Image Classification*, in IEEE Transactions on Geoscience and Remote Sensing, vol. 56, no. 11, pp. 6712-6722, Nov. 2018.

[128] P. Zhou, J. Han, G. Cheng and B. Zhang, *Learning Compact and Discriminative Stacked Autoencoder for Hyperspectral Image Classification*, in IEEE Transactions on Geoscience and Remote Sensing, vol. 57, no. 7, pp. 4823-4833, July 2019.

[129] I. Goodfellow, *Generative adversarial nets*, in Proceedings of NIPS, Montreal, QC, Canada, pp. 2672-2680, 2014.

[130] J. Han, D. Zhang, G. Cheng, L. Guo and J. Ren, *Object Detection in Optical Remote Sensing Images Based on Weakly Supervised Learning and High-Level Feature Learning*, in IEEE Transactions on Geoscience and Remote Sensing, vol. 53, no. 6, pp. 3325-3337, June 2015.

[131] S. Akcay, A. Atapour-Abarghouei and T.P. Breckon, *GANomaly: Semi-supervised Anomaly Detection via Adversarial Training*, In, C. Jawahar, H.Li, G. Mori, K. K. Schindler (eds) Computer Vision-ACCV 2018. Lecture Notes in Computer Science, vol 11363. Springer, Cham.,2018

[132] D. Zhang, J. Han, G. Guo and L. Zhao, *Learning Object Detectors With Semi-Annotated Weak Labels*, in IEEE Transactions on Circuits and Systems for Video Technology, vol. 29, no. 12, pp. 3622-3635, Dec. 2019.

[133] M. Abdelhack, *A Comparison of Data Augmentation Techniques in Training Deep Neural Networks for Satellite Image Classification*. Computer Vision and Pattern Recognition, ArXiv, abs/2003.13502,2020.

[134] M. Y. Saifi, J. Singla and Nikita, *Deep Learning based Framework for Semantic Segmentation of Satellite Images*, 2020 Fourth International Conference on Computing Methodologies and Communication (ICCMC), pp. 369-374, Erode, India, 2020.

[135] L.C.Chen , Y. Zhu , G. Papandreou , F. Schroff , H. Adam, *Encoder-Decoder with Atrous Separable Convolution for Semantic Image Segmentation*. In: Ferrari V., Hebert M., Sminchisescu C., Weiss Y. (eds) Computer Vision - ECCV 2018, Lecture Notes in Computer Science, vol 11211. Springer, Cham, 2018.

[136] S. Sharifzadeh, J. Tata, H. Sharifzadeh , B. Tan, *Farm Area Segmentation in Satellite Images Using DeepLabv3+ Neural Networks*. In: Hammoudi S., Quix C., Bernardino J. (eds) Data Management Technologies and Applications, Communications in Computer and Information Science, vol 1255. Springer, Cham, 2020.

[137] M.C. Younis and E. Keedwell ,*Semantic segmentation on small datasets of satellite images using convolutional neural networks*, Journal of Applied Remote Sensing, vol. 13, no. 4, pp. 046510, 2019.

[138] J. Gonzalez , K. Sankaran , V. Ayma and C. Beltran, *Application of Semantic Segmentation with Few Labels in the Detection of Water Bodies from Perusat-1 Satellite's Images*, IEEE Latin American GRSS and ISPRS Remote Sensing Conference (LAGIRS), pp. 483-487, Santiago, Chile, 2020.

[139] A. Nivaggioli and H. Randrianarivo , *Weakly Supervised Semantic Segmentation of Satellite Images*, 2019 Joint Urban Remote Sensing Event (JURSE), pp. 1-4, Vannes, France, 2019.

[140] T. Ma and A. Zhang, *AffinityNet: Semi-supervised few-shot learning for disease type prediction*, in Proceedings of AAAI Conference on Artificial Intelligence, vol. 33, pp. 1069-1076, 2019.

[141] C. Gonzales and W. Sakla , *Semantic Segmentation of Clouds in Satellite Imagery Using Deep Pre-trained U-Nets*, IEEE Applied Imagery Pattern Recognition Workshop (AIPR), pp. 1-7, Washington, DC, USA, 2019.

[142] M. Aamir, Mohd N. Nawi, , F. Wahid, *A deep contractive autoencoder for solving multiclass classification problems*. Evolutionary Intelligence, Springer, 2020.

[143] M. Barthakur , K. K. Sarma and N. Mastorakis , *Modified Semi-Supervised Adversarial Deep Network and Classifier Combination for Segmentation of Satellite Images*, in IEEE Access, vol. 8, pp. 117972-117985, 2020.

[144] F. Yu and V. Koltun, *Multi-scale context aggregation by dilated convolutions*, in Proceedings International Conference on Learning Representations (ICLR), pp. 1, 2016.

[145] M. Chen, J. Fridrich, M. Goljan, J. Lukas,*Determining image origin and integrity using sensor noise*, in IEEE Transactions on Information Forensics and Security,vol. 3, no. 1, pp. 74-90, 2008.

[146] J. M. Bioucas-Dias, M. A. Figueiredo, *Multiplicative noise removal using variable splitting and constrained optimization*, in IEEE Transaction on Image Processing, vol.19, no. 7 pp. 1720-1730, 2010.

[147] E. Hojman, T. Chaigne, O Solomon, S Gigan, E Bossy, Y. C. Eldar, O. Katz, *Photoacoustic imaging beyond the acoustic difraction-limit with dynamic speckle illumination and sparse joint support recovery*, Optics Express, vol.25, no.5, pp. 4875-4886, 2017.

[148] A. Lucas, M. Iliadis, R. Molina, A. K. Katsaggelos, *Using deep neural networks for inverse problems in imaging: beyond analytical methods*, IEEE Signal Processing Magazine, vol. 35, no. 1, pp. 20-36. 2018.

Lightning Source UK Ltd.
Milton Keynes UK
UKHW010704160223
417122UK00019B/1619